Pain and Purpose

Journey

REV. YOLANDA E. JOHNSON
DR. VIOLA J. MALONE

WESTBOW
PRESS®
A DIVISION OF THOMAS NELSON
& ZONDERVAN

WestBow Press books may be ordered through booksellers or by contacting:

WestBow Press
A Division of Thomas Nelson & Zondervan
1663 Liberty Drive
Bloomington, IN 47403
www.westbowpress.com
844-714-3454

ISBN: 979-8-3850-4059-9 (sc)
ISBN: 979-8-3850-4061-2 (hc)
ISBN: 979-8-3850-4060-5 (e)

Library of Congress Control Number: 2024927135

Print information available on the last page.

WestBow Press rev. date: 12/13/2024

Contents

Foreword

You will be glad you read this work! I write these opening sentences as the current Pastor of both co-authors for over 14 years.

These talented women know life!!! They have had their share of heartaches, including burying loved ones and long-term caregiving. Both are mothers and grandmothers who have experienced the joy of children from birth though adulthood. They are faithful believers in the good news of Jesus Christ. Their faith expresses itself throughout the seasons of life. They are not just hearers of the word, but doers also. As you explore their life journeys through this writing, you will laugh, cry, and pray. You will be inspired to love and live through it all. You might even find yourself being led to worship the God they serve, connect with a worshipping community, and do acts of love.

Have a great read and an even better life because you have read this work by Dr. Viola Malone and Reverend Yolanda Johnson. Blessings to you from a servant of the Risen One.

Cedric Hughes Jones, Jr.
Senior Pastor
The Mount Zion Baptist Church of Philadelphia Facebook@MountZionBC

Foreword

Get ready, get ready get ready, to have a wonderful experience reading about the goodness of God. It is truly an honor and privilege to know women who love the Lord and consistently looking for means that will allow them to share their experiences with others. I have known Dr. Viola and Rev. Yolanda for several years through ministry. Truly a pleasure to know two powerful phenomenal Sisters who want to share with others. They are first-rate examples of "Keeping the faith" as they continue to push through their own private and personal challenges.

They collaborated over many days and nights, pushed through illness and bereavement to complete this book. They are excellent examples of how to: "Be strong and courageous and do the work. Do not be afraid or discouraged, for the Lord God, my God is with you. He will not fail you or forsake you until all the work for the service of the temple of the Lord is finished." 1 Chronicles 28:20. They are devoted Sisters who will continue to serve the Lord in their own way. They have put together a book to address trials and tribulations that we all go through in the flesh and how keeping the faith will bring us through.

Get ready, get ready get ready, settle down in your most comfortable chair, get ready for one-on-one time with God.

Reverend Gail P. Johnson

In Loving Memory of Denice Johnson

Where do we begin? There have been many years of fellowship and fun with our beloved Denice aka Niecy! The beginning of our collective relationship started in 1978, when Yolanda got engaged to a deacon of our local fellowship – Mount Zion Baptist Church. Yolanda was new to our church; however, the Deacon aides (years later the name changed to Deaconess) welcomed her with open arms and that was the beginning of our many years of dealing with life's circumstances. Viola (known as Vye) and Denise had known each other longer from being members of the church before Yolanda; and they started to get closer because of Niecy's parents being a Deacon and Deacon aide along with Elvis and Vye also being a part of the same ministry. As time moved on, we fellowshipped together by going to lunch, dinner, retreats, and other functions as we grew to know one another. Sometimes we would just laugh and talk and just be ourselves having wonderful times! Laughter is good for the soul, and we would laugh especially about life and relationships.

We loved each other and had something different to offer one another.

Denise never had any children of her own, so she took on the role as Aunt Niecy to our children and countless others. She maintained great relationships with all that called her "Aunt Niecy." She always had some form of candy or treats for all of them when they saw her. Niecy always asked her nieces and nephews - "Who loves you?" and they would respond almost simultaneously by saying, "Aunt Niecy," then she would respond by saying "Always remember that!"

Denice had two older brothers and spoke of them often. Niecy was always one to encourage others and proud of any accomplishments of others. She was encouraged to go back to school and finish her Bachelor's degree because of her brother, Reverend Greg Johnson, being a pastor, a husband, and a father with a full-time job. She was also encouraged by her brother's wife, Christine Johnson (whom she fondly called Chris) who always called her quoting scriptures, visiting her in the hospital, encouraging and checking on her, and accompanying Deniece on many appointments.

Niecy was always an open person who loved to give; and that was her way of demonstrating just how much she cared for people. There were times that Niecy would come to us in tears and share the burdens of her heart. We always tried to just have fun and encourage her no matter what her worries were.

We are not sure how Niecy saw herself, but we saw her as a beautiful person with a lot to give to anyone she came in contact with. She was funny, loving, and supportive. Niecy was eager to accomplish her goals and went back to school getting a bachelor's degree and she was involved in many activities within the community and at church.

We believe that she truly loved the Lord and wanted everyone to know it. Niecy loved sharing God's word and truly lived what she preached about. We remember going to the hospital many times to see Denise grateful to the Lord for keeping her here with us. It is so difficult to accept that she is no longer here and when the Lord called her home, it was devastating! Yet, God knows the plans he has for us. So, we are grateful for the times that we did get together – they are precious memories. Words can never express just how much we loved our little sister as we affectionately adopted her as our baby sister in love.

Denise we can say was:

Devoted to her family and friends.
Engaging and empathetic to anyone she knew.
Naturally Nice.
Inspiring messages of her love of God.
Saved by Grace.
Endearing and touched our hearts.
Denise was full of love, caring and compassionate!

Denise was our Sister Beloved!

Reverend Yolanda E. Johnson

Chapter 1

Journey: Pain And Purpose

In the large metropolitan city of Philadelphia comprised of diverse cultures and ethnicities, South Philadelphia a community known for its Italian Market, two families were brought together (against wishes) due to the secret marriage of their children and my parents William H. and Marie E. Martins- Jones. From this union two daughters were born. A few months into their new lives as husband-and-wife, William and Maria confessed that they were married and expecting a child. They apologized to each parent for not requesting their blessing but stated that they knew it would not be accepted. Shocked and upset, both parents voiced their dismay. However, they embraced William and Maria's decision to do the honorable thing and marry. Lorraine was born and a new chapter in the Jones and Martins family evolved.

I wish I could say that all was well with the newly married couple, it was not. William loved to party on the weekends. He would come home drunk and provoke Maria until an argument erupted. Maria loved William however she was getting tired of the alcoholic binges. Never-the-less, she hung in there because William was fine if he was not drinking. In fact, they were having a picnic with some friends at the local park on July fourth, while there, Maria took sick. The friends called for the emergency ambulance to take Maria to the hospital (William and his friends were somewhere in the park playing ball). Later, as William arrived at the hospital, he was taken to the maternity ward to discover that he was to be a father for the second time.

Maria was almost seven months pregnant and because of fibroid cysts did not know (medical technology was not as it is today). I guess you may have figured it out by now, the baby was me, Yolanda E. Jones Johnson. I never considered what it took for the LORD to get me to where I am in life today. However, all of us have a starting point in this journey called life.

As I look back over my life it is amazing to me that I am the age I am while writing this narrative. It is hard to imagine that from the moment of my birth God has truly brought me through many dangers, toils, and snares. I believe what the prophet Jeremiah records (29:11,KJV) "I know the plans I have for you..." God had a divine purpose for my life however it would not come to fruition without pain. As we briefly discuss my journey from pain to purpose, keep in mind that everyone that is born has a divine purpose.

I was born an extremely sick premature (two and a half pounds) baby diagnosed with bronchial asthma. My parents told me that the doctors were not hopeful that I would make it past a week due to the weakness of my lungs and other medical issues. Never-the-less, God had a plan for my life even then. According to my grandmother, I was always in and out of the hospital with asthma attacks to the point that my feet would turn almost blue. She said that God has his hand upon my life because from her perspective, nobody but the LORD kept me alive.

I must believe that what she said was true because throughout my childhood I was very sickly with either asthma attacks, pneumonia, bronchitis, or other upper respiratory illnesses. It is my belief that the stress of being poor and ill-prepared for marriage and having two children (one sickly) in a brief period of time proved too much for my father, resulting in his accelerated drinking habit.

Consequently, staying in the marriage and caring for me until I was seven months and my sister eighteen months, my mother (with her parents help) left her husband to raise their two daughters. My father, sister, and I moved in with his parents until we graduated from high school. Decide for yourself as you read the various adventures experienced throughout my journey in the wilderness of life.

Yolanda Jones Johnson was converted in July 1978, while sitting on a bar stool `at Gert's Lounge, located on the fifteen hundred block of South Street, in Philadelphia.

My father was a bartender for years, upon his retirement from the Naval Hospital. He used to take us to the different bars to meet some of his friends, as a means of showing off his two daughters. These were hard working people that socialized on weekends as a source of relief from their labor. Dad made sure that we knew 'bar etiquette,' which meant do not talk to strangers, and pay for your own beverages. He told us how some of the people could be and to be careful. This was where he spent most of his time for years.

Bars were not a bad place (as far as I was concerned), they were somewhere to meet and socialize with other people). In fact, my friends and (sometime father and sister) I would dress up in our party clothes and go to the bars every Friday or Saturday night until my conversion experience with Christ, which opened my eyes.

One night will never be forgotten. My Father, girlfriends and I went to this club because dad's friends played the band there each weekend. I remember laughing and talking with my father and girlfriends that evening. Something happened to me that I will never forget. I proceeded to take a drink, and it made me sick. All recollect is that my spirit left my body, and I saw myself sitting on the bar stool while others were sitting, dancing, or standing.

Each person was controlled by lines of smoke as if they were marionette puppets. I saw all this as well as myself. Then my life flashed before me like a filmstrip. Once that happened the Holy Spirit spoke to my heart and said, "You do not belong here." Immediately, I came to myself and realized my life would never be the same.

Shortly thereafter, I was inspired to read the Bible. It was as if I was being filled with the very presence of God, while reading. The irony of it is I retained most of what was read. There was such a drastic change in my life that I would pinch myself to see if it were I. After spending three days of fasting and praying and meditating on the scriptures, I was assured that it was the spirit of the LORD doing a work in my life.

Upon my conversion and new life in Christ, I started to attend Bible Study and Prayer Service. People would arise sporadically and share their testimony of what God had done in their lives. After a while, I could not sit down because of the burning desire to tell the church what happened to me. All that I know is I was tired of the world and its disappointments. Immediately after my testimony, one of the Deacons encouraged me to attend the new members Bible Study, which is what, enabled me to grow spiritually.

It is my belief that the Lord called me as a child, but I was afraid to accept the call. I remember asking the Lord to come into the door of my heart at twelve years old. The preacher's, message was derived from Revelation (3:20,KLV) "Behold I stand at the door, and knock; if any man hears my voice, and open the door, I will come into him, and will sup with him, and he with me." The message convinced me to open the door of my heart to the Lord. I wanted Him to know that I opened the door and replied, "Come in." The Lord came and reached out his hand to me, but I was afraid to take it because I thought it meant I would die. It was so real, that as I drafted this essay the picture flashed in my mind.

There have been many times the Lord spoke to my heart amid crises situations, even when He was not "LORD," of my life. There was one occasion whereby someone threatened me at gunpoint, I prayed silently for help. The LORD heard and answered my prayer and delivered me from the hand of the enemy. Immediately the Holy Spirit asked me, "Are you not tired yet?" I was not, because I continued living life my own way until I got tired of making poor choices. It was at that point that I surrendered my life to the authority and Lordship of Jesus Christ in the mid-seventies.

Speaking of the choice to follow the Lord it was in 1978 (not long after my conversion), that while resting and meditating upon scripture, that I had an experience whereas, it sounded like a voice mixed with thunder and lightning that said, "Save the children." It was quite clear and there was a bright light encompassing that voice. I did not understand what was happening to me however, I can see it as part of God's will for my journey from pain to purpose.

Additionally, I developed and implemented several other ministries and organizations to which many Christian leaders are serving in various capacities. The Lord continued to guide me from pain to purpose.

Each phase of spiritual growth occurred whenever I was inspired to read a specific scriptural passage. Moving along in this journey of faith, we can see the hand of the LORD. The Holy Spirit led me to Isaiah chapter fifty-four, various passages illuminated before my eyes. Truly He called me to be his bride and gave me peace and blessed assurance of His love and forgiveness. He was preparing me for ministry to women. Again, it was not long afterward that I saw myself instructing a group of women. Another time I saw myself speaking from a pulpit. It was as if I was sitting in the pew and the Lord elevated me above the pew to where I saw myself speaking. In addition to the spiritual journeys mentioned several others are noteworthy of mention.

I was inspired to read Isaiah chapters, forty-two, and forty-three. The words seemed to illuminate as I read, however, the meaning of each passage served to answer any questions I may have had at the time. Not long after the encounter with scripture people started asking me to be on programs or, short presentations from the scriptures. As the years continued to change there were many significant spiritual encounters. It was when the Holy Spirit guided me to read and study Luke (4:18), that I was convinced the Lord was calling. However, fear held me captive, and I would not acknowledge being called to ministry.

In the mid-eighties I had several debilitating illnesses, at one point the medicine was too strong and it caused me to be paralyzed on my left side for three days. I could not understand what was going on. Not only did I have weird illnesses, but my upper respiratory problems resulted in my having bronchitis attacks, the flu, and walking pneumonia it seemed like around the same time each year. During one crisis when I could not walk because of paralysis of the left side I was inspired to read Psalms (91). It was the Holy Spirit's way of providing comfort.

After being ill for three months I returned to work, in that same week I received a call from a young lady asking me to do a women's retreat. She said that while praying my name was "laid on her heart." This woman had never heard me speak, and I have never functioned as a retreat speaker. I told her that if my husband gave me permission then it must be the Lord's will. While giving her my answer, the Lord laid the book of Esther, on my heart. My husband consented and I did the retreat, and it was a blessing. Can you imagine that I am only giving a synopsis of the many times that I was prompted to step out of my comfort zone?

As time passed one evening while studying, I was guided to read Ephesians (4:1,KJV), "walk worthy of the vocation wherewith you are called." I still did not publicly acknowledge my call to the ministry. Another reason for my reluctance is, my husband did not mind me speaking from time to time, but he was not about to have his wife going around as an evangelist preaching. No way! It was not that he was denying me, but it was the way we both were taught to believe. Never-the-less, he never stopped me from speaking whenever I was asked. Also, I never told anyone of our private conversation as husband and wife.

Once again, the Lord had a purpose and plan for my life and to my shock; I witnessed a change of heart. Here is how it happened; my husband was introducing me as a guest speaker for a banquet one evening about two years after his proclamation. He told the audience that I was a missionary from the heart, and said he believed that the Lord called me, and that I would be preaching the gospel, and be a blessing to many people. I was overwhelmed and grateful to my husband and to the Lord for giving me the wisdom to wait on the Lord's timing.

I still did not acknowledge the call. Truly the patience of the Lord is great! He led me to, 2 Timothy (5:4,KJV) "...do the work of an evangelist..." Praise the Lord. I did not have to tell anybody. All was necessary was obedience to his will and do the work. Not so says the Lord. He led me to Jonah. After reading and meditating on Jonah's journey, I realized that I was running from the LORD's call. And I believe it was not only God calling me, but I was also being sent. There was nothing left to do but continue to allow God to work in my life and strengthen me for the journey.

Therefore, I set a goal to develop in preparation for ministry through academic studies. One evening while preparing for an assignment (which called for developing a project), the Lord reminded me of a ministry that was born in my spirit a few years earlier (1984) called Disgrace to Grace.

Initially, it was planned by one of my daughters and me. It was designed to minister to the needs of hurting women however, it was not time. After about six years the Lord prompted me to develop the ministry in a different format. The revised plan consisted of three phases, first, to have annual retreats designed for families and individuals that have never been exposed to retreats. Next, to develop a Christian Learning Academy, and third to develop a Music Arts after school program.

Phase One of the ministry was organized in (1999) afresh with a new board of directors and with the pastor's permission it was formally birthed as Disgrace to Grace, a 501 c (3) non-profit organization. As the ministry was in the implementation stage, the Lord continued gently wooing me into obedience. The icing on the cake for me was when the Holy Spirit spoke to my heart and said, "Do you love me?" I answered, "Yes Lord." He said, "Feed my sheep." I felt a little strange because I had not been reading that portion of scripture. About fifteen minutes later the same thing happened again.

This time the Holy Spirit, prompted me to tell the pastor. I told my husband first and about a month later told the pastor, which was September 1999. He appreciated that I shared my calling with him and was very encouraging. The pastor also shared his positive views concerning future goals regarding women in the ministry at our local fellowship. I felt relieved once I formally acknowledged my call.

Shortly thereafter, I received a call from a church to be the morning speaker starting their pastor's fifth anniversary. Praise the Lord that was confirmation that it was meant for me to tell the pastor. Also, I got another call to do a revival for women's day at another church and lastly, I received a call to speak at a church banquet. Three calls in one month, all at different churches was final confirmation of my calling and sending.

There are many wonderful instances of the grace of God and favor upon my life in this journey from pain to purpose and, there are times of testing. Are we willing to minister wherever the LORD sends us to? That was our challenge as a couple.

The Holy Spirit prompted me to move into a community where I was raised which changed drastically. The residential make-up consisted of alcoholics, drug addicts, and sometimes violent people. We made up our minds to relocate by faith to where the LORD was sending us. Truly, our prayer life increased and our faith was strengthened. Over time the experience in trusting the divine providence of the LORD, gave me a boldness that was unbelievable. It showed me in those years, just how much false pride, selfishness, and lack of genuine love for people, was in me. I learned how to love the unlovable, but not the things they do. The Holy Spirit enabled me to show love and kindness to the hurting destitute men, women, and children.

After searching my heart and being convicted of ungodly attitudes towards those to whom I am to minister, I had to repent. The Lord, taught me that allowing Him to have free course in my life, enabled me to help some of the young women get off drugs, and began to restore their family life. Each person had a reason for why they chose drugs. For example, one young lady told me that her husband encouraged her to try crack cocaine, because of her yielding to his will she became addicted to cocaine and consequently her family was destroyed, and it resulted in her losing her six children.

This same woman would tell me various stories regarding her life. God had a plan for her life even in her drug addicted condition.

One day the Holy Spirit prompted me to ask her did she wanted dinner. I offered her a good home cooked meal, but she did not want to eat. A few days later I was led to tell her I was praying for her; before I could tell her, she asked me to pray for her. She told me she loved Jesus, and knew He loved her, but the drugs had the best of her. Her story was incredibly sad to the point that I experienced chills while listening. We prayed and I offered to help overcome the circumstances in her life. However, she was not ready to give up the drugs.

One year later she was dead. Someone stabbed her in the same block. She ran down the street bleeding and collapsed on the neighbor's steps next to our home. I was devastated! The lessons learned while living in that neighborhood cannot be taught in a book. Her death brought about a major change in the community.

The various circumstances which occurred during our South Philadelphia mission created a strong desire to culminate my theological studies. Truly, my faith was challenged, however, words cannot express how much I appreciate lessons learned from people that may not be viewed as worthy to be helped. It required faith to allow the LORD, to give me strength to minister to the lost souls in that community and to purpose to prepare academically for His purpose in life.

There is a long way to go but hope is what we by faith believe is what helps us in this journey. I believe that my experiences as a teenager and young woman enabled me to handle the various situations since my conversion. I learned of the Lord, as a child, but was not converted. From my perspective at that time God was my heavenly Father. It was not hard to accept God as father in heaven because my grandmother taught us to pray to our heavenly father, as children. That was important because prayer was my source of strength as a teenager. If the Word of God had not been taught to me from childhood, I would not be where I am today.

The Lord put me through the University of the Holy Spirit! He illuminated His Word and gave me light in my dark soul! I have grown up because the old Yolanda is dead. He changed my entire way of thinking. I believe everything from being a pre-mature baby, my mother not raising us, and all the events up to and including this point, have shaped the call to ministry.

The culmination of my academic journey through seminary was overwhelming, not because of the degree but because it was a precious time from start to finish. I will never forget being in chapel during orientation where we sang Holy, Holy, Holy, the Spirit of the LORD spoke to my heart saying, "You are finally where I want you to be." It was all that I could do to keep from running all over the chapel.

When I graduated, it was the most humbling yet spiritual awakening that God had allowed me to live amidst a disobedient past, to serve him and to receive his stamp of approval Hallelujah! Part of serving the LORD consisted of being patient and doing the work of an evangelist knowing that my sending was from the LORD, and when time for public acknowledgement doors would open.

Shortly thereafter, I acknowledged my call to my former pastor, it was prefaced with "I am not looking for you to license me, I am just acknowledging my call-in obedience to the LORD. I do not expect anything from the church because of its position on women in ministry."

Three years later the former pastor of the church called me into his office and said that he was licensing five women, and I would be one of them. Several months later we were licensed.

Not long thereafter, the pastor was called to another church and almost three years later we called a new pastor. Two years into his pastorate my current pastor the Reverend Cedric Hughes Jones Jr., contacted me regarding ordination as the first woman in the ninety-nine-year history of our church. Once again, I was overwhelmed to the point of tears regarding the purpose and plan that God had for my life. How do I really know that it was of the LORD? Because when I was first converted over forty-three years ago the Holy Spirit let me know that I was going to be the first woman to open doors for other women in my local church. I did not realize it would be ordination.

I am grateful to my Mount Zion Baptist church family for their affirmation and love shown toward me on such an auspicious and momentous occasion in my journey from pain to purpose.

Chapter 2

Journey

Every journey must have a starting point with a specific destination in mind. The same is true for the Believer, it is necessary to know what it took for you to reach whatever age and circumstance you may be in. As a child I used to daydream quite often to the point that life had more to offer than what I was experiencing. God was always on my mind, and I considered him to be my heavenly Father, who I could hold personal conversations with whenever needed.

I remember coming home from church one day with the pastor's sermon vividly on my mind. The church was Friendship Baptist, in Philadelphia Pennsylvania. The pastor sermon was derived from Revelation (3:20, KJV), "Behold I stand at the door and knock, if anyone hears and answers, I will come in and sup with him." I could not get it out of my mind; it was as if it were a record playing continuously.

Later that night when I went to bed, the spirit of the Lord stood in my doorway with His hands stretched out bidding me to come. I wanted to take his hand, but I was afraid that if I did it meant I would die. I believe that was the first real experience of a call in my life. I was twelve years old at the time and it was plain as the nose on my face.

Although I was a member of Friendship my grandmother sent us to another church that was located down the street from where we lived. I loved church and Sunday school, and my desire was to become a missionary due to the influence of a teacher at the Progressive Institutional Baptist Church. She was a faithful and loving teacher whose manner of teaching provoked images of me being on a mission field. The teacher passed away and, I lost motivation to become a missionary.

The Progressive church was in transition due to the teacher's death, and consequent death of the pastor. Therefore, we changed denominational membership. At aged fourteen I joined the Church of God Written in Heaven where the pastor and his wife worked diligently. They were a loving couple, and their warm friendly spirit made me feel as if I was their child. My grandmother was responsible for our attending that church joined along with my sister. I learned more about the Bible, and a term called 'tarrying' (waiting on the Holy Spirit) and praying. Truly, that was a new experience.

We had to "fast' (no eating) all day each Friday and go to church that same evening, get on our knees at the altar and call on the name of Jesus. We would say Jesus, Jesus, Jesus, Jesus, Jesus, repeatedly until you would 'speak in tongues.' I was tongue tied, yet; I looked forward to those Friday experiences. The pastor would preach fire and brimstone messages as if there was no escape. We tried to be responsible Christians because of his preaching. The 'fear' of the Lord remained vivid in our minds! He also required the members to dress in a respectable manner. Women were not allowed to wear sleeveless or short dresses. The length of our dresses was well below the knees, and pants were not to be worn by young ladies.

Overall, the experience was great because of the youth activities. We used to sing in the youth choir. My sister and I sang a duet. I had a lot of devilment in me because I would only sing what I wanted to, other times I would barely open my mouth. My sister used to get angry at me for not obeying her while she would play the piano (as she was trying to get me to sing a different song). The only song that I would sing is, Farther Along (Brad Paisley, Elvis A. Presley), to which I played the piano whenever we would sing that song. One of the reasons for my not singing is that I was shy in front of a lot of people, and the other was that if I was going to sing it had to be what I wanted to sing. Although we would disagree about our duet experience, we had a good relationship as sisters and, with other teenagers in the youth choir. We spent most of our teenage years at the Church of Christ.

My first experience of a boy taking an interest in me was in the same church by a teenage boy who was murdered. He was handsome and seemed to be genuinely nice. I looked forward to going to church even more than ever before. Although we were not allowed to date, it was fun to know that a boy was interested in me. Our parents, both at home and in the church, were extremely strict and did not allow children to be together unattended. Also, the preaching was adamant about sin and damnation that you dare not think or do what was wrong. My sister, who is eleven months older, made sure that Tommy treated me with respect in church, and for him not to ask me for a date because I was too young. She also put the fear of my father in him! We never went on a date; however, it was the very first time I began to think about boys in a new way.

Around the age of 14 to 15 I was sitting on my backyard steps gazing at the sky, seeking God for answers. My teenage cousin was killed. Why did he allow my 16-year-old cousin to die? Suddenly, it was as if the sky became brighter, the clouds began to form letters as if it were handwriting for me to read. The rays from the sun were beautiful and as the clouds began to come together, they formed a footprint. To this very day it would be extremely hard for anyone to convince me otherwise. A sense of comfort filled my heart that day, and I was able to face the events leading up to and including the funeral for my cousin. The word ministry was not used much in my fellowship circle but, the term "witness' was. We had to warn people that they were going to hell if they did not repent and live holy. Also, we would caution them not to read the book of Revelation because according to their belief, readers would be cursed! Also, the world was ending. I did this about three years straight until it dawned on me (with the help of new friends), that reading Revelation was a blessing the world was 'not' ending. Consequently, I began to change my way of thinking and living. From the ages sixteen through twenty-seven my life was like a roller coaster, I went from spending most of my time in church, to frequenting worldly places. Church attendance became less frequent as the worldly lifestyle seemed more appealing. Although I enjoyed the party life, there was a nagging thought about God in my mind. One time it was clear to me while at a party, the Holy Spirit, spoke to my heart and said, "Aren't you tired yet?' I did not take heed. The company I kept was not who my parents desired me to associate with, but rebellion was predominate in my life and I did what I wanted to do. This resulted in a long-term relationship with a young man who never attended church and did not view God in his economy. It turned out to be over eight years of turmoil, and stressful living with me having two children (out of wedlock). I believe that God allowed my rebellious lifestyle to be a catalyst to provoke me to establish a relationship with him that was 'real' and tangible.

The Christian foundation was set during early years with a childhood view of God, but the intimate relationship was developed during the chaotic stages of my life which caused me to cry out to the Lord for help. It was not easy raising children as a single parent, but it was the consequence for the fruit of my ways, and I was responsible to provide a living for my children. Also, the Lord let me have children to give me opportunity to think about others more than myself. I was vain thinking that I was the prettiest woman out there, and when things did not go my way, I was 'not' nice. Some people said that I was quite mean!

The school of hard knocks taught me that I was not all there was to life. By the age of twenty-seven, I started attending the Most Blessed Sacrament Church because my children attended its school system. I was highly active in their school and became trained as a certified teacher's assistant. I taught in their elementary school for over two years. It was during that time that I studied with the priest for nine weeks to become a catholic. I had one more class to complete to fulfill requirements of becoming catholic, God has a way of redirecting our paths!

After attending mass, the Sunday prior to the final session, the Holy Spirit guided me, directly to Mount Zion Baptist Church. It was as if a Geiger counter was leading me, I will never forget that experience. What blew my mind is, when the then pastor of Mount Zion, preached, it was as if he was talking directly to me, all the questions I asked the Lord on my knees in prayer the night before, were answered. I joined Mount Zion that day and contacted the Catholic priest soon thereafter letting him know, I returned to the original denomination of my childhood. This experience proved to be the turning point of my life.

Shortly thereafter, I started attending Bible study, prayer meetings, and Sunday school on a regular basis. Although I did these things, my life had not completely changed. As the old saying goes, I had "one foot in and one foot out" of the church. Then, one night I went to prayer service and found myself giving a testimony. I do not remember all that I said, but one lady told me that I had the church in an uproar of praise because I was tired of the world and I knew that the Lord had his hand on my life, and that I wanted to serve Him for the rest of my life. That was the true spiritual turning point of my life. I have never been the same since!

Praise the Lord! I know the Lord started dealing with me again during those years because one night as plain as the nose on my face, the loud voice which sounded like thunder said, "Save the children." There was a radiant light that went with it. At the time I did not equate it with a call of God on my life, but I knew that I had to work with children.

Another quite interesting thing happened to me in 1978 when I was in an environment that I should not have been in. While sitting on a barstool (and before purchasing a drink) at a local tavern, my spirit left my body, and I could see myself in a real sense. Everyone around me was either laughing and talking or dancing. The amazing thing is that each person had smoke screens or lines of smoke controlling the moveable parts of their bodies, as if they were strings that control marionette puppets. Suddenly a film strip of my life appeared before me and a voice said, "You don't belong here." After such a real event I came to myself at that moment, and said goodbye to those with me, and I went home. I never went out to the night club or taverns again.

The year 1979 presented yet another interesting experience while on my knees praying because of some unkind actions directed to me by some folk at church. The Holy Spirit prompted me to read the book of Isaiah chapter fifty-four. Certain passages illuminated as if a bright light was shining down on the words itself. One thing for sure is that when I finished reading the entire chapter of Isaiah a deep peace engulfed me and a secure confident feeling of love from 'my heavenly

Father. In retrospect that was a call from God to peace and divine direction for the rest of my life.

I continued to thirst for knowledge of God's word. Therefore, I began to write or study little messages every time the Lord would impress scriptures on my heart. At other times II Timothy chapter two, Isaiah chapters 40, 42, and 58 were given to me by the Holy Spirit. Next, I was directed to read Luke 4:18 to which I did a private study which led me to Isaiah 61. While studying these passages I visualized the war between the Lord and Satan. All around them were desolate places and the realization that Lucifer exalted himself above God. At that point I saw the glorious power of God and suddenly, a sense of total unworthiness overtook me, and I began to repent afresh (not because of any known sin) but, because I experienced the holiness of an awesome God.

Once I repented and yielded myself to God afresh, music welled up in my spirit as if it were an angelic choir and orchestra. Suddenly, a voice said "Write!" The words 'He came to set the captive free' were sung by the choir along with other verses to which I wrote. What a glorious experience. I gave the music and song to some musicians that I know and the only time I sing it is when the Holy Spirit inspires me to do so.

He came to set the captive free,
He died for you and me—
Don't you see His hand of love,
Sent down from God above?
He died, now I 'm alive,
Because He came to set the captive free.
I'm free, Halleluia, I'm free.
You know He came to set the captive free.
He died now I'm alive because,
He came to set the captive free.

Several months later I experienced a life changing experience while reading the gospel of John, in one setting. Again, I was praying specifically for the healing of a tumor that I was supposed to have removed, but I did not want to go through another operation. I happened to be watching the seven hundred club and decided to pray with the person that was praying for the television audience. While on my knees it was as if radiation went over my body and the hovering presence of the Holy Spirit. I knew at that point that my body was healed.

Reading the gospel of Saint John in one setting produced results that changed my life forever. Never have I read anything that transformed my life such as the book of John. It was as if I was observing the various events with my own eyes. When Jesus called Lazarus from the dead, I sensed the pain that Jesus must have felt because He knew that Lazarus would be coming back to a world full of sinful people only to suffer and die again. He also knew that death had no dominion over Him, but for the eyewitnesses to know that death is not final as they believed, but it was considered sleep as stated in John.

Ironically, the fear of death left me once I completed that segment of scripture. Most of my life I had a serious fear of death, especially since I was asthmatic and suffered quite a bit. Also, there were many tragic deaths in our family including an axe slaying of my cousin and her two children. Another healing experience regarding death and the issue of it being 'sleep' in Jesus, was a sermon that I heard at teen-aged friend of mine's funeral. The preacher said, "He's not dead, he just asleep." I was truly angry at the preacher for that statement, how could he say such a thing?

The fear of death gripped me over the years as I saw tragedy, sickness, and death at an early age. It is unbelievable what I was experiencing while reading. It was as If I were on a dusty wilderness plain with houses such as is depicted on most pictures trying to depict the times of Christ. I could see silhouettes of Jesus calling Lazarus from the grave while crowds stood watching. It was like I was on a journey traveling with an itinerate preacher whose assignment was concluding.

Finally, I got to the passage that gives an account of Jesus going to the cross; it was as if I was in that crowd walking towards Golgotha's hill. What turmoil! It was very intense and grave at the same time. The anticipation of what is about to take place. Jesus being nailed to the cross, the agony he experienced, the shock and horror. I felt as if I could see Mary moaning for her son enduring such brutality.

The women wailing while men hung their heads and some cringed in total dismay. I cried bitterly as if I would never stop. It was like I was a baby needing to be consoled by her mother. The agony of it all. He was on the cross fulfilling his Father's will to be obedient even unto his death on the cross.

Once Jesus gave up the ghost the crowd began to dissemble, and folk proceeded homeward. Disbelief, abandonment, anger, many emotions that take place when a loved one dies. Days of weeping took place during this virtual reading experience but, it was all at the same time.

An amazing thing happened as I journeyed to the tomb with Mary and Martha and found that it was empty. I started to laugh uncontrollably and rejoice. It was unbelievable what I was going through. You would have had to experience that for yourself to understand what I mean (and not think that I was hallucinating). My biggest regret was that I did not journal what happened at the time that it took place.

Once again, the Lord impressed upon my heart to read Revelation chapter (3, KJV). It was quite vivid that He wanted me to "hear what the Spirit saith to the church." The question is what was he trying to teach me? Was he saying listen to me or hear what I have to say? Or was he telling me to return to my first love, namely Him (Jesus)?

Surely the implication was that He loved me before I ever loved him, but at one time I did absolutely love him and turned away from him. Therefore, he was calling me back to himself. It was quite difficult for me to acknowledge that the Lord called me because of fear. I was ashamed of my past life before Christ and some of the events that had taken place.

Exposing the moral weakness in my life to my children was exceedingly difficult but I had to confess to them and tell them about the grace of God in my life and how he could use me as a witness of that grace. As time went on people would ask me to participate in various functions either to give the welcome address or a short spiritual message. In 1984, I was asked to speak at a women's retreat, which was held at the Blue Mountain Christian Retreat Center located in New Ringgold, Pennsylvania.

The final confirmation that I was to do the retreat came the day of departure when I was on my way to work with my bags so that I could be ready to leave immediately afterward. When I got off the train, I realized that I left the bag home with the material I prepared for the weekend. I began to panic first and then I prayed as I walked toward my job. I said Lord, what am I going to do? I left all the work at home.

Not long thereafter a beautiful thought came to my mind that let me know that I should trust Him. The following is how the Lord spoke to my heart in answer to prayer:

E is for eternal
S is for salvation
T is for trinity
H is for holiness
E is for everlasting
R is for redemption

When that thought was completed the music and words Redeemed, Redeemed, redeemed by the blood of the Lamb. Redeemed, Redeemed, his child and forever I am(Frances Jane Crosby. author), welled up in my spirit until I started singing. I knew everything was going to be okay, and it was.

A year later I was asked to do a house fellowship to which the Lord gave me Acts (1:8, KJV) to research and write a message on. The title of the message was 'Prosperity and the Home.' During that time, my husband and I had a beautiful home but were contemplating selling it to purchase a smaller house. The Lord spoke to my heart and directed me to move back to an area I did not want to live in. The message convinced me so much that I told my husband to which he said no way would he move in that neighborhood. Now it is obvious that if the Lord really wants you to do something he will allow things to happen that will help you do what he wants.

Different circumstances took place that provoked us to decide to move where we did not want to move. One event was that my father was stabbed in the house where the Lord wanted us to live. There has never been anyone to break into that house in the more than fifty years that my family lived there. Do you know what happened the night my father was hurt?

When my husband and I went to clean the house and see about my father, the Holy Spirit spoke to my heart and said, "I want you here!" It was quite clear. Also, at the same time my husband said "Yo," I believe we can bring mom back and live here awhile." Little did I know that the Lord was using those events to answer my grandmothers' prayer and the desire of her heart to come back home where she would be with her son.

The experience that night was one never to forget because my sister met us at the house and said "Yoyo' (nickname), you and Richard could stay here, after all you do not have any small children." That was the final confirmation. We humbled ourselves, sold our house (in four days) and moved. The Lord wasted no time in helping us to make up our minds. Earlier I said that I wanted to be a missionary as a young girl, this was the first 'mission field' project that the Lord assigned.

The same night of the stabbing and making the decision to move also came with a specific mission to minister to five souls on that block. The Lord laid the names of five people on my heart to share his gospel, which was another indication that this is where the Lord wanted us to live. What a mission!

Wouldn't it be nice if I could say that everything was peaches and cream, moving from a suburban type setting to the inner-city drug infested neighborhood where prostitutes advertised their bodies on street corners? There was a sense of peace in my spirit primarily because I knew that we were in the will of the Lord; but my husband commented that he did not know if we would be able to live there very long.

My reply to him was to remember a previous commitment that we made to the Lord as a couple that we wanted to be his missionaries, and that this move was our mission. Truly it was at that point that I realized that the Lord had fulfilled the desire to be a missionary in my life. Not only in that circumstance but it caused me to look over the various projects that the Lord has allowed in my life and to see that call come into fruition.

The five souls that I mentioned earlier gave their hearts to the Lord. Those souls consisted of drug pushers, drug users, and prostitutes. It was unbelievable! The Lord used the fact that I knew and went to school with the parents of the new babes in Christ, because as a child I grew up in that community and in the house that the Lord prompted us to move into. The difference in the community was shocking due to the decline in moral and family values. The neighbors kept the block clean and knew each other, and they did not allow negative influences control where they lived.

Most of the families attended church or some religious organization, and it was a safe environment to raise your children. The economic factor was mostly low-income, but it was not used as an excuse to tear down a community. People lived within their means and used tools such as paint and cleaning agents to keep their property in decent shape. The picture is much clearer as to why the Lord allowed us to move in that location. When my sister (Lorraine) and I were young we were called the 'Jones" sisters, or those 'church girls' who could not do what the other children did (for the most part).

We were the first ones in at night since we could not be out after dust and the other children except for one or two families did not go to church. Consequently, we were teased quite a bit. But we knew the parents and those parents told their children about us and how that our neighborhood was like a family. Once we moved in, the siblings (who were the five souls) lived in the houses that their parents owned, and they treated us as if they had known us for a long time.

Although their parents were children of the sixties like me, the difference between us was that Christ was the foundation in our family, and the other children's families' foundation was crime. Since we moved on that block the Lord had given us boldness to witness and lead souls to Christ. Some have moved, died, or gone to jail. The girls that used to sell their bodies have changed locations. I remember telling them that if I had lived in the house that they would stand in front of (since it was a corner house) they would not be allowed to stand there.

The lady was a prisoner in her own house because she was afraid to report them or chase them away for fear of repercussion. Guess what? The lady died a year later! Her niece had her cremated within three days before the neighbors knew that she had died. The ironic thing is that when I was a little girl, I used to wish that we could live in that house because it was nice, and it seemed so big. I guess you can figure out why I made that statement. You are right! The niece who was the heir of the deceased and a childhood friend of mine, called me while I was at work and left a message with my husband about the death of her aunt, and the offer for us to buy the house. Unbelievable, isn't it? That is how the Lord works.

We do not have to seek a mission he will guide us to it and prepare everything that is necessary for us to do the work. We purchased the house and moved, shortly thereafter. The move could not have come at a better time because it had become quite difficult to continue living in the house we were in because my grandmother had gone home to be with the Lord and her son (my father) was living in the house and being taken advantage of by some of the prostitutes who would ring the bell or call him until he would open the door.

One of their specialties was to prey on single male senior citizens who are lonely. On one occasion after returning from vacation one of the 'pipers' (crack addicts) as they were called, was in my kitchen cooking. That was the last straw. The Lord knows how much you could take, and I had enough of trying to keep the peace in my home while dealing with the prostitutes and my father. Once we moved into the house the campaign began for me to get the girls off the corner.

I would share Christ with them and approach them with the conviction of a mother who would encourage their children to strive for a better way of life. I did not want them to feel that I was casting judgment on them but appealing to their heart with an attitude of love and concern.

There was a young lady, who used to frequent the corners that I talked to each time she would make the mistake of sitting on the steps (to promote her services) who one day started to light her crack pipe with a young man that was with her in broad daylight. She did not expect me to be home because we were away on vacation (each year we would go away for about a month or two in the summer). She and the person were surprised that they were caught. I said to the young lady, "Don't you think you are getting quite bold?" She grabbed up her paraphernalia and they both ran around the corner.

Approximately one-half hour later she rings my doorbell and attempts to explain her behavior. She said that she was married but her husband left her with their six children who devastated her to the point that she gave up on life and her family. This young lady began to use crack cocaine which became an addictive habit that was so bad that she did not have the strength or desire to get off it. She apologized for smoking it in public and that I saw her. Her profound confession was that she knew that Jesus loved her and that she loved him also, but she could not help herself.

As she confessed her love for the Lord and her regret for what she had done along with the trauma in her life, chill bumps came on my arms because I felt her pain and a deep since of compassion overwhelmed me as we talked. I remember trying to encourage her heart and help, but she said that she would be okay. A few weeks later I saw her and offered her dinner because of the prompting of the Holy Spirit. She did not accept the offer but thanked me for asking. The following Sunday the Lord laid it on my heart to pray for her as my husband and I were on our way to church. Before I could say anything to her such as I am praying for you, she said, "Ms. Yolanda, would you pray for me today? I told her that the Lord had inspired me to pray for her and that I would and invited her to attend church with me sometime.

The next Sunday she was dead! What a tragedy, her throat was cut on a Saturday evening in a house located up the street on the same block where we reside. She ran down the street to the house next door to where we used to live with my father, and the residents called the police. She was pronounced dead as they arrived at the hospital, but she was able to say who stabbed her. I was devastated upon receiving the news concerning her murder. The only consolation to me was that I was obedient in sharing Christ with her and hearing her confession of faith. Her flesh was delivered to Satan for destruction, but her soul was saved. Her death opened the door for a greater witness.

The neighborhood has not been the same, other Christians took an active interest in the community and worked diligently to gain more control of their neighborhood. The police implemented programs to ensure more safety and less open crime and prostitution as a result. That was one of the many incidents over the years of our tenure in South Philadelphia. God's mission field is usually not something or someplace that we would want to do, or go, but it is best to obey his call regardless of what we feel, as the blessings are insurmountable.

The next mission was in financial services. One day I went into the credit union at our church to complete a loan that was granted; the officer asked did I want credit disability insurance, and I said no. He told me that I had to take it, and I told him that it was not mandatory. We had a long debate in which the treasurer asked me did I wanted to work there. I thought he was kidding but he said since I had experience in financial services, they could use the help. Although I was licensed in that area, I had no idea of how to operate a credit union. I took advantage of the training and other resources available, and the Lord remained faithful to the mission designed for me while serving in that capacity for seven years.

Most people do not see secular work as a mission, but it is. We are to glorify the Lord in all that we do and seek his wisdom before making major business decisions. During my employment at the credit union, I began to sense that the Lord was prompting me to go to Eastern Theological Seminary. It was vivid in my mind, no one had discussed that organization with me. I was enrolled at Liberty University at the time and decided to continue with that program.

The Lord sent me two faithful and honest trustworthy workers who daily gave their time and talent to this ministry. I believe it was to free me up to be ready to move on to my next assignment. By this time, I realized that the ministries that the Lord assigned were usually temporary. I completed my tenure with the credit union in October of 1997 and by January of 1998 I was asked to join the newly formed counseling ministry of our local assembly (Mount Zion Baptist Church).

In June of that same year, I was asked to accept the position as pastoral counselor. What confirmation of the Lord's hand in my life and his divine guidance. He put me in a ministry once again which I did not pursue. Consequently, I researched what the position required and set forth to meet the qualifications. I took continuing pastoral education at the University of Penn Health Systems. I became a chaplain and certified in pastoral counseling at Geneva College. Also, earning a Bachelor of Science degree in developing urban ministry leadership. To God be the glory for wonderful things He has done.

Do you remember that I said that I was afraid to tell people that I knew the Lord had called me into his service? The question is why am I acknowledging it now? My answer is due to the events that took place prompting me to do so. For about a week the Lord impressed my spirit to read the book of Jonah. Each day, I would read until I was confident that the Lord was assuring me with a warning that he was sending me, and I was rebelling. It was comfortable to serve the Lord in whatever capacity 'I' wanted to serve. After I told my husband of my conviction while studying the book of Jonah, I received an invitation to do a women's retreat for Harambe Baptist Church, to which the subject was 'A Vessel of Honor.'

What a blessing it was to minister with another woman whose subject correlated with mine. That is one way the Holy Spirit confirms his word and allows a ministry to come together when it is bathed in prayer.

My next to the oldest stepdaughter and some of my sisters in Christ, attended the retreat with me and the Lord really blessed. An interesting thing happened toward the conclusion of the retreat; I was asked to give the altar call after we presented the message. What an experience! The Holy Spirit spoke to my heart concerning a hospital ministry for one lady and something else for another. I remember explaining to them that this was new for me, and it was not something that I normally do but tried being obedient to the leadership of the Holy Spirit.

The Lord was truly faithful in that the women acknowledged that they were convicted by what was declared and the Lord had spoken to their heart about the specific ministries prophetically spoken. There was a time when I thought that when people would say that the Lord was speaking to someone's heart concerning specific ministry's that it was phony. Now I can attest to the reality of faith in God and what it means in to mean in a real and tangible sense.

Upon reflection of what the essence is of God, I cannot help but reflect on the Spirit, which is a divine substance that motivates me toward active faith. I believe God's presence is felt or sensed yet it cannot be touched. God is the substance of my faith and the evidence in my spirit that he exists. I believe that Scripture affirms and strengthens my faith. I believe and I know that God is real and that he changed me! I believe in the power of God's love through the demonstration on the cross. Faith is the only way I can comprehend and believe in the riches of his love. Demonstration for our sins.

Historically, God has over a thousand names Yahweh, El Shaddai, Jehovah-Jireh to name a few. People have many expressions of who God is to them and it is personal. God is in the box of humanity, but God cannot be boxed. He is too big, and he is awesome. He is a mighty God, a Fortress, a Rock, a strong Deliverer; He is the Omnipotent One, the Omnipresent One, and the Omniscient One. He is the King and Sovereign One. He is God alone! I cannot know God apart from his divine revelation of himself therefore, I must believe that God through the sacred pages of scripture identified his attributes and character.

Through Jesus Christ the kindness and veracity of humanity was demonstrated. By the power of the Holy Spirit the confirmation of who God is, has been confirmed in my life and I now along with many clouds of witnesses affirm God's existence. Without faith I cannot know God; with faith I can love God and know that I have a relationship with God, because of Jesus Christ. Faith is hearing the Word of God and believing it and acting on that belief which is what I did.

I believe that God called me to do the work of an evangelist by the power of the Holy Spirit and through the redemptive work of Christ on Calvary. He gave me a hunger and thirst after righteousness and a love for humankind with a desire that all should know God in the pardon of their sins.

Whereas I was not as confident in ministering initially as I continued in the study of the Word, Bible study and consistent worship services my faith enabled me to witness as a good soldier of Jesus Christ should. It is an awesome responsibility to serve the Lord or to know that the God of this universe, the Creator and Sovereign One chose me and fellow witnesses' to be a voice in the wilderness of 'other's' lives that they may hear the Gospel, receive it, and be saved. Home missions is the first work God gave me to do in that the Holy Spirit prompted me to have Bible study in the home and next service in the church as a Sunday School teacher.

Serving the Lord is an honor and privilege God bestows on those who are willing to deny self and to pick up their crosses to follow Christ. Those who choose to serve the Lord must be thoroughly trained to do the work and must walk in accordance with biblical teaching. I believe servants of God must walk circumspect, in this world and be accountable for their actions. Trained ministers of the Gospel whether ordained or lay should exhibit love and be willing to put the good of others before themselves.

Chapter 3

Dementia Caregiver

Our beloved friend and brother in the Lord, wrote this poem which is befitting for seniors. It is how I viewed my Richard.

**The senior example by remember Donovan
Reverend Jerry Sanders, Author**

I spend a lot of time with seniors.
And it breaks my heart.
To see the struggles, they must endure
Dailey, from the start
Some of them are bedridden.
And every day is the same.
Some of them are wheelchair bound.
Some make it with a cane.
Some are pushed and some are pulled.
But all of them are game.
As I observed their fortitude
And their determination
To wring out every drop of life
Without exasperation
I thank God that I can stand and walk.
Without aid, on my two feet

Because of their example
I never contemplate defeat.
I will keep on keeping on.
I will follow their steadfast lead.
I will trust in God, just as they do.
To satisfy my needs.

Today, January 21ˢᵗ, 2023, was overwhelming; Richard was walking backwards and forwards talking about heaven and out of his head. No matter what I did to try to help him to lay down he wouldn't do it and then he was in his mood. When he gets like that, I like to try and see what I can do to help him but not agitate him. Sometimes he can be stubborn and does not like to be told what to do.

His behavior was quite difficult so, I had to lay down and ask the Lord to help calm me. It dawned on me to pray that the LORD give him Peace of Mind. Shortly thereafter, the Lord answered my prayers by calming him down and giving him a peaceful attitude letting me give him something to eat! There were so many different things happening and getting bad news about various ones put him in a very bad state. I guess all that at one time just became a bit much.

I had to focus on self-care. I thank the Lord I just said wait a minute this is too much I cannot handle this; I must lay down and I thought about the scripture that says in quietness and confidence shall be your strength. A beloved friend gave me a plaque years ago which reads, "In quietness and confidence shall be your strength" Isaiah (30:15,KJV). It truly blessed my soul and that is what I thought about today as I was anxious.

I was afraid today mainly because I did not know what was happening with Richard. It was scary I know as old as I am every day that we wake up above ground we are blessed to be on this side a little while longer however live with the reality that this is still temporary. Truly taking care of him-no matter what mood he gets in is a learning experience. It is not about me; it is about providing the best care for him recognizing that even where he is at, he's probably wondering what's wrong with him.

It could be quite frustrating for him nevertheless he makes the best of it, and I praise God for that. He walked backwards and forwards for exercise because he used to be unstable so for that I just say thank you, thank you, thank you Lord.

I have learned to gauge where he may be mentally sometimes, he's just like a little baby and wants to be held but whatever I know it's my responsibility to try to help him. I am grateful that he is happy and expresses his happiness.

Hopefully, this will help some dementia patient caregivers to study the position and figure out where they are mentally. It may be good to look at the distinct phases that a person goes through. One thing is certain, God has equipped me and those who place their trust in Him, to endure inconvenient situations in life.

Chapter 4

Endurance

2 Timothy 2:1-3 (ASV) 1 Thou therefore, my child, be strengthened in the grace that is in Christ Jesus. 2 And the things which thou hast heard from me among many witnesses, the same commit thou to faithful men, who shall be able to teach others also. 3 Suffer hardship with me, as a good soldier of Christ Jesus.

The two letters to Timothy and the one to Titus are labeled Pastoral Epistles. They were written by Paul to two of his young converts) who had followed him on many of his missionary journeys and whom he had established as pastors of churches at the time of the writing of these epistles. Although they were addressed by Paul to his young friends in the ministry, the message is for churches. The apostle Paul in these past epistles gives instructions to his son Timothy in the ministry. My parents taught me right from wrong. They provided examples of possible consequences that could result due to wrong choices. It was up to me to adhere to their teachings or pay the price of disobedience. In like manner Paul admonishes and exhorts Timothy to conduct himself as a young minister. His letters are guidelines to leadership in the household of faith as well. Nearing the end of his life, Paul, while in prison, wanted to give Timothy some final instructions face to face, he realized that he may never leave prison alive. Therefore, his main plea is for Timothy to 'come.' He needed to see the familiar face of a loved one. Timothy was truly beloved by Paul who knew his life would soon be over. He went down memory lane mentioning Timothy's grandmother Lois and his mother Eunice regarding their faith. That was interesting to me because of the influence of each loved one. It is a blessing to have godly parents or in Timothy's case his grandmother and mother because of their influence on his life. Parents see what we don't, they may see character traits in our lives that were either in them or other relatives that was their desire for us. Paul perceived that Timothy had faith like them. His father was Greek and not recognized as a person of faith. Paul reminded Timothy to stir up the gift of God or to live like what he had been taught and ordained to do by Paul's commissioning with the laying on of hands. Just in case Timothy was afraid to minister Paul let him know that God had not given him a spirit of fear, but of power, and of love, and of a sound mind (2 Timothy 1:7, KJV). This instruction Paul gives Timothy is also a reminder to us. What has God-given? Love! God has given us unconditional love and demonstrated by giving his only son Jesus as the satisfaction for our sins. Jesus was the sacrificial lamb for you and me. Just think about the word sacrificial meaning designed to be used up or destroyed in fulfilling a purpose or function. Paul wanted to assure Timothy that he did not have to be afraid because God had equipped him with power, love, and a sound mind. He did not want Timothy to keep quiet about what the Lord had done for him or for what the Lord would do or has done for others. Are you afraid to give testimony to the Lord? Do you know that you do not have to live in fear? Are you secure in your love for the Lord because of God's love to you? Please, know that you have a sound mind, and nothing can shake that foundation if you believe God has equipped you.

What do we mean by equipped? Acts let us know, *"but you shall receive power after that the Holy Ghost has come upon you; And you shall be witnesses unto me both in Jerusalem, and in all Judaea, and in Samaria, and until the uttermost part of the earth." (Acts 1:8, KJV).* The Holy Spirit has equipped us or empowered us to be witnesses for the LORD. Part of our witness is to endure hardness as a good soldier of Christ Jesus. All of us have or have had things in our lives that seem unbearable. Sometimes we might question what is next or how much more can I take? Yet

Paul says to endure hardness or hold up under whatever it is you are going through as a good soldier. Paul was quite familiar with The Roman soldiers who were resilient, disciplined, and considered the most resourceful soldiers in the world. They marched twenty miles a day with fifty pounds of gear. When they were not in active war they practiced as if they were. A good soldier does not quit because of difficult tasks or a dangerous situation. They understand their life is expendable and they must be prepared to lay it down when required. This is part of what Paul is calling Timothy to—stay in the battle regardless of what takes place. How we handle life's difficulties indicates what type of soldier we are. Suffer hardship with me, as a good soldier of Christ Jesus. The new King James version says, "you must endure hardness as a good soldier of Jesus Christ."

> **Endure:** undergo, go through, live through, experience, meet, encounter; cope with, deal with, face,

> **Hardness:** the quality or state of being hard.

(2 Timothy 3:11, KJV) Persecutions, afflictions, which came unto me at Antioch, at Iconium, at Lystra; what persecutions I endured: but out of [them] all the Lord delivered me. Paul says, with me, in other words I am not telling you to do something I have not done or not doing. Look at where he was! Prison, a damp dungeon, nothing like today. Yet, Paul was concerned about doing the work God called him to do. He was able to remember that the LORD delivered him out of them all. Do you remember the many times God delivered you? I do, some have been shared earlier. Are you sure that He will do it again? Although it may not be easy, we are going to be encouraged to endure. The times we are living in are unprecedented for most of us. The pandemic, George Floyd around the same time, new variants of COVID, and murders everyday throughout the country. Mass shootings, the list goes on. Notwithstanding, our own firsthand experiences. Suffering, tribulation all sorts of chaos yet Paul says to suffer hardship with me as a good soldier of Christ Jesus. Why should we be glad to endure hardship as Jesus Christ? Because He set the example on our behalf. He did not

know sin, but He became sin for you and me. Therefore, we need to do what Hebrews (12:2 KJV) Says, "Looking unto Jesus the author and finisher of [our] faith, who for the joy that was set before him endured the cross, despising the shame, and is set down at the right hand of the throne of God." For the joy that was set before him! Mercy! He endured the cross knowing the outcome yet, for the joy…of being able to sit with the Father, His Father.

Widowhood

As I sit here in September 2023 pondering my life from birth up until this point seventy-seven years. I am a recent Widow. My husband of forty-three years passed away in May as a matter-of-fact May 7th, 2023, he was 2 weeks shy of being 90 years old. What could I really say? Of course, I miss him, no one welcomes death, but we can rejoice in knowing that he lived past the time promised. Three score plus ten which is seventy; anything beyond that is a bonus. What was I going to do? How was/is the rest of my life going to be? For over 43 years we did about everything together. Now I need to remember that God will see me through the years ahead. I questioned where did the years go? Immediately, the Lyrics of a song (Hold to God's Unchanging Hand (Jennie B. Wilson, Franklin L Eiland) reminded me that, "Time is filled with swift transition…in other words time waits on no one.

Recognizing that life is fleeting, my goal should be to "Build your (my) hope on things eternal…hold to God's unchanging hand (Jennie Wilson, Text)." The many years of married life to a precious soul like Richard is a dream many women have. He was a kind and loving husband whose main goal was to love and provide for his family. We met in church. I was new to the congregation and required to attend New Members class. He was the teacher. Although I was in his class for about 6 to 8 weeks, he recognized my zeal for the Lord and recommended that I go to Bible school.

New Life Bible Institute was newly formed at Beulah Baptist Church. It was my first experience attending that type of school. I was richly blessed and could not wait to attend each class.

As I ponder over that period of my life I can remember when I was in Richard's class (known as Deacon Johnson), sometimes he would refer to his wife as having gone home. I thought that meant she went down South! In my past relationship, my friend and I would go down south which was called going home each summer to visit loved ones. It was not until a few months later that on the first Sunday, which was a communion service, that one of the men at Mount Zion approached me with a compliment, saying that they were grateful for the missionary work that I was doing with the young people.

I said thank you, he said Sister Jones, a good Christian woman like you should have a Christian companion and, there is two men in the church that are single, one is on the choir and the other just lost his wife. He said Deacon Johnson lost his wife, but he never gave me the other fellow's name! I found that remarkably interesting. Nevertheless, I was upset because I did not go to church to try to find a man and I did not really appreciate anyone trying to set me up with somebody.

So, I said to him thank you so much for the compliment, but I did not come to church to find a man. I do not know what you are thinking about. I did not look for a man in the world and I certainly did not come to church to look for a man. One thing about me is my grandmother that raised us always said that if you have a problem or something that you needed to take care of and needs to be addressed, always go to the horse's mouth. I decided to go and look up Deacon Johnson's name in the telephone directory. Several questions needed answers, why would someone give me his name? I never did get an answer why someone would be trying to match me up with him. I did not know the person who approached me other than seeing him at church. I never had a conversation with him or anyone else about Deacon Johnson. It was not something that I would do. Dating was the farthest thing for my mind because I was focused on growing spiritually.

I was upset! Upon finding Deacon Johnson's number, I decided later that evening to call. When I spoke to Deacon Johnson, he said that he was sitting upstairs, thinking about his children and the fun that they were having but he said that I was on his mind. He would never have known how to call me.

Let me backup for a moment when he answered the phone I said hello Deacon Johnson this is Yolanda Jones calling I got your number out of the telephone directory because I had something on my mind and my grandmother always told me that if I had an issue to go to the horse's mouth and right now, I am calling you because I am upset. I do not know what is going on, but I did not come to church to look for a man and one of the men in the church today said that that was a deacon that lost his wife and gave your name.

Deacon Johnson said that he did not know anything about anyone trying to arrange a relationship for him. Deacon Johnson said he would not have known what to do, he said he had been married for 23 years and his wife had passed away. His comment was interesting; I said I remembered in the class you said something about your wife that went home! I thought going home meant down South. In my family and friends when people said, we were going home, or they are going home that meant they were going down South to visit loved ones. I acknowledged that I understood what he meant, and I expressed regret. That is how our communication began.

One thing that I can remember to give a little context of history is, I used to sell dinners and baked sweet potato pies. People at church would purchase dinners to include one of his friends who was coming to get dinner and a pie. I never paid any attention to it because again it just would not have been he was not someone that I would have would have looked at as far as a relationship. He seemed like a nice man, but he was an older person, and I looked at him as a teacher. No way did I think that somewhere down the road he was going to be in my life.

I was fully dedicated to the Lord and had an encounter with the Lord that I might have said earlier in one of my chapters, but I said that I remember it's like the Lord backed me up against the wall and said who are you going to serve God or man? I knew that it was at this point that I had to decide to choose the Lord. It was choosing life or choose death and probably end up being dead, so I chose the Lord, and I thank the Lord.

I dedicated my mind, my will, my soul, and my body to the Lord. Also, at that point of conversion or transformation I never was one to do much dating, but I also knew that even in dating I didn't have to run a football field to know what it looked like. I value myself and I feel that I am queen of my ship, and I was good looking, and I was narcissistic and probably still have a lot of those traits today. I said I was fine then, and I am fine now just I'm Gourmet! Thank the Lord, I was 31 years old at the time. My new relationship with the Lord was fantastic. It was a new way of life, peace, joy, just the sense of belonging to the one who redeemed me. All I could do was praise the Lord and learn as much as I could about the Lord at that time. I made so many bad decisions I was tired of the world, tired of smiling on the outside and hurting on the inside. No one can give you peace and joy on the inner man but God. Happiness is a momentary emotion of feeling but Joy is long lasting. This joy that I have in the Lord is because of the blood of Jesus Christ! I thank the Lord and was not about to jeopardize my relationship with the Lord or my testimony of the powerful Deliverance that God wrought In My Life by coming to church looking for a relationship.

The only focus I had was the Lord Jesus Christ. I wanted to grow in grace and knowledge of my Lord and Savior because it was new to me yes, I was a Christian, I grew up in the church, but I didn't know the Lord. The type of encounter that I had, I did not want to disappoint my heavenly father for looking out for me. I will go back to continue what I was saying earlier about the phone call. It was amazing because as we communicated, he told me about his children and that he had a beautiful life, but his wife had died of cancer.

He asked me how school was, I said that I really enjoyed it and was grateful. He asked if he would if it would be possible to pick me up from school the next evening, I said yes and it's really interesting because it was a refreshing conversation no nothing out of the way just a nice conversation but it's so unbelievable the next evening he picked me up from school was on Monday evening, do you not know that this man asked to marry me? It was deep! I think I must have been out of my mind.

He asked to marry me; he said the Lord showed him me; this was too deep for me! However, the wildest thing about it is I said yes before I knew it. Before I could really think too good something in my gut seemed to force a yes out of my mouth and that was too deep for me. I literally wrote that in my diary at that time and unfortunately did not know that I was going to be writing my story although I had always said I would keep it there I lost all my manuscripts.

I lost a lot of things that I wrote so I'm just rewriting from memory what I could it's so much that I'm missing but that's a moment in time that I will never forget. My husband was not playing, he was just nice. I believe it because he was nice, that's why I said yes. This is not me I would have thought he's just spontaneous.

Who asks someone to marry them on the first (not even a) date? He was only picking me up from school. He said it was night and maybe safe to have someone pick me up, that was too deep for me. I really smile each time I think about it, look at God. We don't know why things happen the way that they do (especially when it's a new thing), all we must do is make sure that our trust and dependence is on the Lord. I'm sitting here 45 years later to include the courtship; I still smile at that early time of meeting in our lives.

That is how our relationship started. Fast forward, as we started to develop a friendship, we laughed, we talked and went through our courtship which consisted of going to visit the sick for my church because he was a deacon. I Marveled at how he ministered to people who were sick, it was a wonderful learning experience.

First, and most importantly learning that faith is all about learning who God is, what God has done, how he did it and who Jesus Christ is. What did Jesus do, who is the Holy Spirit. Why is it so important? I believe learning how to live life based on principles derived from the word of God helps build strong family and friend relationships. I remember as a child most parents went or sent their children to church. They had faith which might have been weak, but they wanted to make sure that their families were strong and had faith.

We prayed in the home and had Bible reading. The little gospel books of Matthew, Mark, Luke, John, and Proverbs were in just about every household. Children in the last couple of generations have been influenced by social media. They get so involved in the games which introduces them to levels of violence. They would play war games always killing and disrespecting the police and authority. Negative things are going into young people's minds.

I was blessed although I had two children out of wedlock, I was not proud of it because my parents taught no children before you get married. In fact, no sex before you get married. I went around with my head hanging down for a long time. When I look at God's plan for my life if I had been married, he would not have given me a second thought. I never thought about how much my husband went through just to date me and subsequently, become my husband.

Chapter 5

Change

First Kings chapter one provided insights that enabled me to establish family relationships in a new way. In hindsight, I think about the way I was raised and realize my parents did the best they could as my guardians. However, growing up for me was difficult and family relationships were volatile. I imagine the struggles and hardships I have endured perked my interest in the story of Solomon. I wanted to see how David's instruction to his son Solomon could have benefited my parents. My paternal grandmother that raised me did not go past a sixth-grade education, but her wisdom taught us how to live. She taught us to respect God and ourselves. She gave us the tools to survive. I thank the Lord, that my heritage may not be royalty, but in Christ we are royal!

David's story provides understanding of the high expectation placed upon Solomon, his son, to fulfill his responsibility as an heir to the throne; and I see how our lives should reflect what it means to be heirs. As a child of God, I am an heir to all that Jesus promised those who follow Him. I also have a responsibility to fulfil the lofty expectations of my family (my grandmother and my dad) of me.

I think of the many conversations we have had and how they gave me guidance as a parent/guardian. This is no different than David preparing to die and telling his son, Solomon to be strong and to be a man. His father gave him some words of wisdom which I think is the normal thing that a parent would do.

I wonder if Solomon was thinking that he was strong, that he was a man, and wondering what his father was implying? I was reminded the Apostle Paul said, be strong in the Lord and in the power of his might, put on the whole armor of God that you may be able to stand against the Wiles of the devil (Ephesians 6:13, KJV). We need to be mindful that Satan's job is to kill, steal and to destroy our testimony. Sin is easy for humans because it is our nature. We need help. The Holy Spirit is our helper. Just like Eve was tempted by the Serpent in Genesis (3 KJV) while Adam was with her and did nothing but disobey God's command by eating the forbidden fruit. Humankind does the very same thing today.

For his father to tell Solomon to be strong lets me know that he may be talking about strength in another way. And we must realize that too much of anything will weaken you and impair your capacity to think properly. Therefore, be a man! Don't get so weak with worldly things that you make decisions that are foolish.

David is telling Solomon to keep charge of God and be obedient to God's laws, to know his laws, understand his laws understand the instructions that God has given down throughout the generations. If David gives instruction to his son, how could those instructions help me? I believe learning what God's laws are and striving to be obedient will help me to be blessed by God the way that Solomon was advised by his father.

David wanted his son to be strong and be a man not just any man but a man that represents the Kingdom. My question is why was it important for Solomon to understand the importance of being obedient to God's commandments, his judgments, and the testimonies? I believe it is important for me to understand that if Solomon was required to adhere to God's Laws, then it is just as important for me to obey the LORD'S command if I want to be blessed because Solomon is an example of receiving the blessings of obedience.

David told Solomon that in doing so, God would prosper him in all his ways wherever he went. Also, God promised David that if his children took heed to follow in the path set before them by God, the

House of God that David wanted to build but God said no however he would allow it to be built if David's children followed a path that God set before them.

King Solomon loved the Lord, walking in the statues of David his father; only he sacrificed and burnt incense in high places (1Kings 3:3, KJV). The Lord was really pleased with Solomon even to the point the scripture says, the Lord appeared to Solomon in a dream saying, "Ask what I shall give thee." Solomon continues by saying, you have made me King, but I am but a little child; I know not how to go out or come in; there are a lot of people to serve (1 Kings 3:6-9,KJV).

I can imagine that Solomon being given such an awesome responsibility as a young man was overwhelming. My situation is not like Solomon's, however, the rules and regulations given to me by my parents seemed too much to bear. We couldn't have fun like the children in our community because strict limitations were placed on who we could play with and how long we could be outside. We were instructed to be a witness for the LORD, and to memorize scripture to share with others. That was a lot because I didn't fully understand most of it myself.

Solomon had a huge task and said wait a minute I'm a kid, I'm young. I don't know what I want. How many young people have said - I don't know what I want. When I was young, I made a bunch of dumb mistakes, but in this case let's look at what king Solomon said, I need help!

He is falling on the mercy of God he is saying thank you! I appreciate your offering me everything, but I need help with your people I don't know how to rule these people. God these are your people; I'm too young to be in this position. How many times have loved ones passed and maybe children had to raise their younger siblings. They were not King's kids, they were not born with a silver spoon in their mouth, a gold spoon or whatever they might have had a plastic spoon so they just did the best they could.

I remember prior to getting married, I made some decisions but the decisions I made were primarily to take care of my family. But look at God even though Solomon was young he wasn't too young to recognize that he needed help. Material things were not going to help him, he needed wisdom in how to handle the people. God asked him a basic question What do you want? What can I do for you? When you think about it Solomon asks for something that money cannot buy. He asked for wisdom, not only did he ask for wisdom he asked for understanding and how to apply that wisdom.

Therefore, Solomon does what James instructs us to do as Believers. "If anybody lacks wisdom let him ask of God who gives freely and does not hold back (James 1:5, KJV)." Only ask God! "He said give therefore thy servant an understanding heart to judge thy people that I may discern between good and bad; for who is able to judge this so great a people"? God granted his request (1 Kings 3:9,10,KJV).

When we stop and think about what it meant for Solomon to ask for wisdom and understanding most often, we wouldn't think that that could mean some serious issues had to happen for answers to be given how in the world would we know if we have wisdom if we don't have anything to test that wisdom by?

Have you ever had a situation take place where you didn't know how you wanted to handle it? Sometimes you pray for understanding and wisdom. It's very hard to believe that a holy and righteous sovereign God, creator of the heavens and earth, waits for us to ask! The Epistle of James states, "if any man lacks wisdom let him ask of God (James 1:5,KJV)." He doesn't hold back he freely gives but the question is, do we believe? I remember how painful it was raising the children as a single parent. My life was in danger at one point, I didn't know what to do and I was tired of being intimidated, concerned that somebody was stalking me or going to shoot me.

Finally, I had to trust God for my life. I had to ask the Lord to remove evil forces from around me. I couldn't walk around in fear, so I had to ask for wisdom and guidance and understanding how to take each day at a time raising two children. God heard my cry and answered, thank you Lord.

Just as the Lord allowed major crisis to happen in my life that would cause me to ask for guidance, Psalm (32:8,KJV), reminded me that God says, I would teach you and guide the way which I would. I prayed to the Lord and He would give wisdom as to what to do but it would always be behind a crisis. In other words, the storms of life had to hit me so that I could be able to ask God for wisdom.

Solomon was no different he had to be tested in areas of wisdom how would he know that God had granted him wisdom if a test did not come his way So what happened? The text says it happened, when Solomon was old that his wives turned away his heart after other Gods; and his heart was not perfect with the Lord his God, as was the heart of David his father.

Solomon was not quite like his father and had his own issues to deal with. He was at a crossroads; God was not pleased as the text says, The Lord was angry with Solomon because Solomon disobeyed. Once I heard a pastor say, "Sin will take you places you did not want to go, make you stay longer than you want to stay, and pay a price you did not want to pay." the price of disobedience.

Disobedience has consequences, we must pay the price but, it does not mean that God forgets about us. He loves us, that is why we are chastised. We love our children, sometimes we must punish them because of disobedience. Consider some of the young people that are shooting, killing, and maiming each other while doing all sorts of things that are unheard of why is that? I believe it has to do with parenting and lack of godly wisdom.

Think about how Solomon in his youth asked God for wisdom and understanding, God answered his request and gave him wisdom how to handle certain situations, one of them was two wives had babies at the same time one died both claimed to be the mother. Solomon had to decide who was telling the truth. Solomon had the child brought to him and instructed the child to be cut in half. The woman that wasn't the mother didn't care, but the mother said, "no it's hers!' Solomon was able to identify that mother because he knew that only a mother would make a sacrifice like she did. God gave him wisdom and understanding on how to handle difficult situations consequently, he became well-known for his wisdom and understanding.

Ecclesiastes is one of the many writings of wisdom literature of Solomon's that can help us understand how we as humans think. In this first chapter Solomon, named himself as the preacher in verse one as, the Son of David, King of Jerusalem. I wonder was his identifying as a preacher or teacher and chapter one was because of the lessons in life that he learned. I know myself looking back on my life and thanking

God for being able to reach the age that I am I have learned a lot. I've learned that as smart as I thought I was, I was not as smart as I thought. If we're not cautious even in the Lord, we make some foolish decisions. I am so grateful that at this stage in my life I do not feel like Solomon may have felt. Solomon's journey through life concluded that it is "Vanity of vanity (Ecclesiastes 2, KJV)" asking the question what profit has a man of all his labor which he takes under the sun (2:22, KJV)? SUN! He was in deep thought. Life was good. He was the son of a king. Never had to worry about the necessities of life such as you and I. Yet, he concludes that life is empty or as some may say useless.

Can you imagine Solomon had everything he needed but he did not have true love. He had material goods that did not make him happy, he had a lot of wives and concubines that did not make him happy, he had a lot of wisdom as well as understanding but, he was not happy. He was missing the most crucial element of life and that is first and foremost knowing and loving the one who created you.

I remember loving the Lord as a child and preaching and warning everyone I encountered about fire and brimstone for those who do not know the Lord. I didn't want them to go to hell. As I grew older, I fell in love with the world and my conversation changed. I developed a world philosophy and stopped trusting in the word of God. I am grateful God got a hold of me and gave me an opportunity to get to know him in a tangible way. Solomon had everything yet he was miserable. He had questions about life. Do you ask questions like some of us have asked? Why did we have to be born only to be miserable?" His search for meaning or happiness and gaining wisdom in every area of Life resulted in abundant grief.

The more he learned the more sorrowful he felt. Solomon decided to evaluate life in Pursuit of Happiness and pleasure; he concluded that all is vanity and vexation of spirit (2:17, KJV). What does it mean to be vain? The noun for vanity means excessive pride. What does the synonym for vanity mean? Conceit, conceitedness, self-conceit, narcissism, self-love, self-admiration, and self-regard. In other words, life says that everybody is for themselves, everybody wants their own thing including himself. What about vexation? What does it mean? Vexation is the state of being annoyed, frustrated, or worried. That is the noun form the synonym says annoyance, irritation, irritability, exasperation, anger, rage, fury, temper etcetera. In other words when a person is self-absorbed, and things don't go their way they're going to be upset we're going to be upset if it's us we're going to be annoyed with things we're going to be irritable, we're going to be angry.

I made my own decisions. I chose the path that I took therefore, I had to pay the price. Sometimes, we don't always understand that some choices made are a consequence of what was happening. Solomon conceded these things because he had done just about everything. The wisdom and understanding given to him; the average person doesn't have. Consequently, life is not what he desires. He built vineyards, Gardens, Orchards, anything he needed or wanted he was able to do or to get done but with all that his conclusion "All was vanity and vexation of spirit and there was no profit under the sun (2:17, KJV). SUN! He focused on wisdom, Madness and folly and asked the question "what can the man do that comes after The King?" With all his wisdom and exploits in life Solomon hated it because everything done under the sun brought him grief and was "vanity and vexation of spirit (2:26, KJV)".

Solomon's Pursuit of Happiness what did it get him?

We can ask a question as we look back over our lives: What did we pursue? saying, all I want to do is be happy; like the song says Don't Worry Be Happy(Bobby McFerrin, Author). Pursuing happiness brought me heartache and pain, but Pursuing God bought my redemption through the blood of my Lord and Savior Jesus Christ. Salvation in Christ Jesus has given me joy. *The joy of the LORD is my strength (Neh. 8:10).*

Acknowledgements

I am grateful to God for every aspect of my life because through it all, the good as well as the painful situations enabled me to trust explicitly that every Word of God is true.

What would I have done without my parents and my sister who did what they had to do to raise me, I am grateful. I love and praise God for my two beautiful biological daughters who always loved me and seemed to accept my bad and good times unconditionally. I thank them for supporting me when I made the decision to get married. Words cannot express the love and gratitude that I have for my husband who loved and accepted me and my children unconditionally. I love and thank the LORD for my four beautiful Stepdaughters who loved and respected their father so much that at a very painful time in their lives they accepted me in their lives as we grew to love and appreciate each other.

What could I say but thank you and much love to all my twenty-one grandchildren to include our grandson who preceded Poppop in death. We had some wonderful times together never to be forgotten. My loving great grandchildren, what can I say but I love you and appreciate all twenty-six of you. Some have been able to be around us more as well as to help with Poppop and I nevertheless all are loved equally.

Thanks to all my family, friends, and loved ones especially my Mount Zion Family. Each pastor and ministerial staff were instrumental in my spiritual growth and development. The Deacons and Deaconess board and every auxiliary of the church is a power testament to the goodness and grace of God in people's lives and how they serve God's people in various capacities. You will never know how much I really appreciate each one of you.

To my Disgrace to Grace Family, thank you for your unconditional love over 25 years. I love all my mother's (Mama Bear), Older Sisters and mentors, you know who you are.

Pastor Cedric Hughes Jones, Jr. Words cannot express the gratitude I have for not only creating history in Mount Zion Baptist Church by ordaining me as their first woman clergy in its 99-year history but always supporting me in ministry. Also, I am grateful for the wonderful foreword penned in this book. Thank you.

Reverend Gail Johnson, it is with gratitude that from the moment I met you our spirits connected in a bond of love. Your humility and dedication and support has enabled me to make some especially important decisions. Thank you for the beautiful and motivating foreword written in this book.

I am grateful and full of love for my dear friend co-authoring this brief synopsis of our lives and inspiring words to hopefully provide encouragement to its readers. Thank you, Dr. Viola J. Malone, a mighty woman of God, empowered by the Holy Spirit to endure hardness as a good soldier of Jesus Christ. I admire your strength as a Woman, Wife, Mother, Grandmother, and friend.

Thank you, Yolanda Malone-Bates (aka Little Yolanda), for editing this work amidst your busy schedule and for the loving way you did it. Truly, I appreciate it because I am not the best writer (smile).

If I missed anyone please charge to my head and not to my heart, there is a reason we did not add all the names of people and loved ones. Please know that we appreciate you.

References

Chapter One

Jeremiah records (29:11,KJV)
Revelation (3:20,KJV)
Isaiah chapter (54)
Isaiah chapters, (42,43)
Luke (4:18)
Psalms (91)
Esther
Ephesians (4:1,KJV)
2 Timothy (5:4,KJV)
Jonah

Chapter Two

Revelation (3:20, KJV)
W. Stevens (1938). Farther Along
Revelation
II Timothy (2)
Isaiah (40, 42, 58)
Luke (4:18)
Isaiah (61)
John

Revelation (3)
F. Crosby (1882). Redeemed
Acts (1:8, KJV)
Jonah

Chapter Three

Isaiah (30:15,KJV)

Chapter Four

2 Timothy 2:1-3, ASV
1 Timothy 1:2, ASV
Titus 1:4, ASV
2 Timothy 1:7, KJV
Acts 1:8, KJV
2 Timothy 3:11, KJV
Hebrews 12:2, KJV
Wilson, J., F. Eiland F. (1906). Hold to God's Unchanging Hand.
Matthew
Mark
Luke
John
Proverbs

Chapter 5

1 Kings (1)
Ephesians 6:13, (KJV)
Genesis 3 (KJV)
1Kings 3:3, (KJV)
1 Kings 3:6-9, (KJV)
James 1:5, (KJV)
1 Kings 3:9,10,KJV)
James 1:5, (KJV)
Psalm 32:8, (KJV)
Ecclesiastes

Ecclesiastes 2, 2:22, 2:17, 2:26, (KJV)
B. McFerrin (1988). Don't Worry, Be Happy. W. Pharrell (2014). Don't Worry Be Happy
Nehemiah 8:10 (KJV)

Dr. Viola J. Malone

Chapter 6

Humble Beginnings

"From the rising of the sun unto the going down
of the same - the Lord's name is to be praised"
Psalm 113:3 (King James Version).

What a marvelous way to begin a chapter in a book. Truly, God has been my refuge from the time of my birth, and He will continue to be until the time of my demise. Had it not been for the Lord keeping me since my early existence, it would not be possible to pen this book's chapters. Let us begin this journey of my life – showing some of the ways God has been forever present in my life.

A little African American girl, born mid-day on a Thursday in November to two loving parents - Bill and Ella Mae (Guy) Jackson. I was the seventh child of nine children born into poverty in a small rural area of Arkansas. The first four children (Eugene, George, Gilbert, and Emma) were born at Dean's Island known now as Osceola, Arkansas – a part of Edward's Plantation. The next four children (Larlene, Carlton, Viola, and Rosie) were born in Chelford, Arkansas now known as Joiner, Arkansas. The last child born to this union, Henrietta (was actually a twin, according to her birth certificate, but the other child did not make it, and its gender was unknown). They (the twins) were born in Whitten, Arkansas. The names of our places of birth have changed because over time the land owners changed, and so did the name of the town. As for us, the Jacksons, we were all named after my father's or my mother's brothers and sisters as their way of showing respect to family.

I was told by my parents and older siblings that I was born in the hands of a midwife, who took care of my mother during her pregnancy and coached her through all of her child births. I was born small and alert, calm for only a second until all types of ruckus came from me, as revealed to me over the years. My older siblings were very protective of me – I guess from us being so close in age spreading two to twelve years apart. We were a close-knit family that did almost everything together – we went to church together, we played made up games, and we told made up stories to entertain each other day in and day out. We could pick and choose what we wanted to do for our entertainment, however, we did not actually have a choice about going to church. It was a must!

Every Sunday, we attended church services all day. We started with Sunday School, regular church service, and then Baptist Training Union (BTU). There was also something called Red Circle – which required us to remember Bible verses and recite them. As a child, this was a lot for me and all so boring (at least at the time). It seemed like the adults were comfortable "Praising the Lord" – All Day! I believe during the time of my youth, we were denied many of the opportunities that the White children had, such as access to extracurricular activities, swimming pools and the like. So, to our advantage, we had God on our side, and we learned to trust His guidance. It seemed easy to follow our parents' example and the adult leadership of church members simply because we did not have anything else. All-in-all, now as an adult, I am grateful for those experiences as a child and all that God has done in my life, continuously. It makes me understand the song "Grateful" by Hezekiah Walker.

I guess God was always being instilled in me and it was just a matter of time for me to seek Him out for myself. As I mentioned, we (my family along with extended family) did everything together including church. As a result of us attending multiple services over time, this led to a greater experience in my life's journey. I can imagine for any child all day church may seem boring because it seemed boring to me, my siblings, and my friends - who were in our age group. Please let the record show that church was mandatory, and all church services were a must. No church, no play!

One evening my family and friends were invited to a Revival. The first couple of nights some that attended revival were saved, but I did not welcome the invitation to accept Christ. I did not take the Revival seriously until the third night. That night, my best friend and I were on the mourner's bench (a section/bench where people sat and prayed to seek salvation - similar to an altar call), and two elderly women in the church were. praying for us…They were praying that we would get to know Christ. I remember what the lady was saying. "Ask Jesus to save you and come into your heart." So, I repeated those.

words from her, as I was told to do, and initially, I was fearful of what others thought as they watched. But He touched me is an understatement. Considering the lyrics of the song "He Touched Me" by William Gaither. My friend and I both recited the words, and we raised our hands. Before long, I felt a wave of peace come over me and I was no longer fearful. Instead, I was encouraged to know my family and friends were there to witness what was happening. I was only eleven years old, but I knew it was the Spirit of the Lord, and I became a believer in the Lord Jesus Christ. ·

James 5:16 "The effectual fervent prayer of a righteous man availeth much" (KJV).

The next phase of my life's journey was to be Baptized. What an experience! We did not have modern pools like today. My experience of baptism opened my eyes to grace and mercy. It was early in the morning during Sunrise Service by the river. A number of parishioners gathered to Baptize me along with others who accepted Christ as their Saviour and those who were already saved. During my baptism, I did not know why the men/elders of the church went into the shallow part of the river with sticks to beat the water. I was filled with fear of the water, but I did not know the reason for literally treading the water with sticks was to assure that the snakes would flee, if any were there. Surely, my fear of the water would have been heightened had I known that snakes were visitors of the water. Again, God was a Refuge.

Psalm 46:1 - "God is our refuge and strength, a very present help in trouble" (KJV).

Bill

My dad (Bill) was a medium height, thin man, that meant business when he spoke and had to say very little when he did speak. He was a quiet, no-nonsense man who loved his children, and was definitely not a disciplinarian by any means in my eyes. At least, I do not ever remember him administering any type of discipline to me or my siblings. In fact, he was kind and gentle to all of us, yet stern and insistent upon us learning how to keep house and earn a living. This is not to say that he did not discipline us at all, however, as stated, I don't remember any sort of correctional intervention on his behalf.

According to my brother, Gilbert, our grandpa, John, my dad's dad - had 18 kids and married 3 times; and my grandmother (his first wife) had a twin sister. Twins run throughout my blood line and seem to have skipped a generation until my great niece had twins a few years ago. Anyway, I never had a chance to meet my grandfather nor my grandmother. She preceded my grandfather in death, and he died while my mother was pregnant with me. I believe she died during childbirth.

I do, however, have many fond memories of my dad, and I love him for all that he has done to show us right from wrong. For instance, one memory off hand was - on a hot summer day near the beginning of the school year, my dad took me and my younger sisters to the nearest town (a very small town with a total population probably about 80 people) to purchase shoes from the only shoe store owned and operated by white management. We all had flip-flops on, as usual because it was summer. So, it was hard to determine our shoe sizes for enclosed shoes without being fitted properly. Be mindful that this era in time was still during segregation which I will continue to state as I reminisce of different times during the 40s. The white shoe salesman met us at the door and very sarcastically inquired. "What can I do for you, boy?" My dad replied, "I want to buy shoes for my children." The salesman asked my dad, "What size shoes do you need?" It amazes me as I write that this is still quite a painful memory to share through any form of dialogue or expression (verbally to discuss and even just to type). My dad seemed saddened, and I am not sure if it was because he did not know our sizes or because we were stopped at the door confronted by a white man - like he was superior to my dad. I wish I truly knew what he was thinking; and I wish he knew he was still the greatest in my eyes. Unfortunately, no one of color was allowed to try on the shoes prior to purchasing them in the South and I could see the hurt look on my dad's face as we stood outside the store. Therefore, I immediately said, "Daddy I know my size."

Thinking that would possibly speed up the process; and of course, I did not know anything about shoe sizes. So, I took responsibility for my dad purchasing a pair of shoes that were probably one size too small at least for me. And I dare not tell my dad that the shoes were too small. You may be wondering if I kept those shoes and the answer is, Yes! I wore those shoes until they were so tattered and torn, they had to be discarded. You can imagine that my next pair of shoes were one size too big, and I could not run in those shoes. So, I learned to walk slowly - like a lady. Lifting my feet so high, in today's time it would appear that I was showing off a pair of expensive "red bottom shoes." Actually, I was trying to keep those big shoes from falling off my feet.

Ella Mae

My mother, affectionately called "Mama" was a beautiful woman, small in stature, but so strong. She also knew you had to work hard to make things happen. Mama was a homemaker that raised her children and challenged all of us to be the best at whatever we could do. She showed us how to sew, crochet, cook, and even to farm the land (to help my dad). So many spring and summer months, my siblings and I had to chop cotton from sun-up to sun-down; and in the fall and early winter months we picked cotton. During my youth, many Whites owned the land in the south - while the African Americans labored hard, long hours for as little as $2.50 a day from 6am to 6pm to till the land. To me, slavery did not seem so far off looking at the way we worked.

"He that tilleth his land shall be satisfied with bread: But he that followeth vain persons is void of understanding"- Proverbs 12:11 (KJV).

Those long days working in the fields showed me how to appreciate my family, especially my parents, and the lessons we learned through them. My family had so little in comparison to some, but our unity, love and devotion for each other and God was immeasurable. We undoubtedly lived in poverty, and many wonder why have so many children, what is the need for having a large family especially if you are living in poverty? The answer is two-fold: loving parents that loved each other and loved sharing their love of the Lord and seeing God through their children. They believed God would provide and take care of all of their needs. In spite of having to struggle to put food on the table, as well as in the ice box (a box-shaped gadget that stored items before electric refrigeration). Some poor people could not afford modern appliances. My parents knew the power of prayer, hard work, and perseverance. Times were so hard, yet my mom and dad showed us how to be appreciative of even the smallest things. So many times, now more than ever I know the meaning of Shirley Caesar's song *"I Remember Mama."*

Another explanation for having a large family would simply be because during this time, there was a lack of knowledge and experience with birth control and not many conversations about a woman's body. Another reason to explain the rationale could possibly be from people just not having knowledge of financial wealth and only knowing and stressing the importance of having an education. To some - more children meant more people to help out around the house and in the fields doing farm labor. My dad worked as a sharecropper – a free person who is allowed to live in the property on the land owned by another person as long as the farming of the crops is being maintained by the "renter". Needless to say, the white owners made millions of dollars from the cheap labor from the African Americans working. There were never equal plains between the races.

We lived in a small rural area known as Chelford, Arkansas which was predominantly segregated by class and race. Most people have never heard of this place. Therefore, here is a little geography for those still wondering, "Where in the world is Chelford?" It is located approximately fifty miles Southwest of Memphis, Tennessee; and Arkansas itself.

is Northeast of the state of Texas. Hopefully, that allows you to pinpoint this area of the south - the southern part of the United States.

I can remember two homes we lived in when I was a child. The one I remember the most was a 2-story four-bedroom house that sat back off the dirt road tucked between tall trees and plenty of locust and mosquitoes. There was a living room, a kitchen and two bedrooms on the first floor; and there were two bedrooms upstairs. The bathroom was really an outhouse (an outdoor toilet) because it was outside the main house. During this time, the only people that had access to indoor toilets were the more affluent families. It wasn't too often anyone would venture outside to use the bathroom during the night. For the evening, many people used a chamber pot. When I was growing up, we did not have electrical wiring in the house, nor did we have gas heaters or stoves. For the most part, kerosene lamps were used for lighting and wood was used for heating the house.

The house seemed large at the time with two floors. Day in and day out we spent quality time with family and extended family near and not so near. We read schoolbooks and played games from the books we read. We listened to music on the radio, and went to bed before 10:00 pm, and sometimes as early as 8:30 or 9:00 pm. Usually, earlier bedtimes were because we had to go to school or work. The girls slept in one bedroom, and the boys slept in another bedroom. My oldest sister, Emma, stayed with my Aunt Larlene (my mother's oldest sister) and my youngest sister (Henrietta) slept with my parents. My mother and father always stayed downstairs in the living room in order to keep a watchful eye of the house, as well as to be able to hear if anyone should try to creep up the steps.

Psalms 91:" The Lord is my light and my salvation of whom shall I fear" (KJV).

Needless to say, God looked out for all of us, and no such wickedness of outsiders barging in ever happened. We slept safe and sound, but that did not stop fear from entering into the minds of children. Keep in mind that an exceptional dreamer dreams beyond the natural realities of life and possibilities. I was always dreaming.

I remember as a young dreamer, thinking that I would purchase my parents a home some day with all the amenities other families had. Amenities such as indoor bathrooms - instead of an outdoor water pump, electricity running throughout the house, and gas heating throughout the home, as well. I often dreamed about being able to own a doll because I never experienced receiving a toy for Christmas when

I was little. We always enjoyed fresh fruit and cakes of our choice. Our Christmas was a humbling experience, indeed. I dreamed of having a house with more rooms than anyone could ever imagine; with food in the ice box running over; and I dreamed of having so many dresses and shoes I would lose count. Dreams were just childish dreams and ways to avoid the reality that life was hard.

The disparities among the African American families were great compared to the White families and systemic racism was overt. Housing, education, and economics are just a few of the disparities that existed amongst the African American and White families.

All children in the community were bused to their segregated schools. African American children were bused to attend Wilson Trade School, in Wilson, Arkansas. I (along with many others) was bused from Joiner, Arkansas to Bassett, Arkansas, then from Bassett to Wilson, Arkansas. I remember being told countless times white children had new books, swimming pools, and other amenities while the African American children received used books. I do not remember ever having a fresh, new book during elementary nor high school. I just remember working hard and trying to learn as much as I could. As a result of my arduous work ethic, I was 12 years old when I went to high school; and I graduated when I was 16 years old from high school.

While in high school, I also met my future husband, Elvis, and we were friends my entire four years of high school. (I will speak more on my husband in Family and Friends). Being in high school gave me a new experience because I was only 12 yrs old and high school students ranged in ages from 14-19 years old. So, I didn't really fit in well with some students because of my young age and lack of secular knowledge. However, it was an advantage having older siblings because they were protective of me, and my innocence and we did homework together which allowed me to advance academically. As you would expect, I learned a lot being around my older siblings and older students at school.

As mentioned, my older three brothers did not have the same opportunities as my younger brother, sisters, and me. They had to drop out of school in order to help out with supporting the family. For the most part, the older siblings of many African American families (like in my family) had to drop out from school in order to aid and maintain family structure and housing upkeep. We (me and my siblings) were always respectful to all people, especially adults. So, for my brothers to do this was just another way to show respect for their family and parents. Marvin Sapp explained it best in his song, *"I Never Would Have Made it"*.... *so only God knows how we made it!*

It seemed unfair to me that they had to sacrifice their education until later years to help support the family just from being the oldest of the nine of us. My youngest brother, Carlton, is the only male sibling that finished high school. He later joined the Army, and we were all so proud of him being in the Armed Forces. My older brothers did farm labor jobs and later took on their own families. I always looked up to my brothers because they helped to provide food and shelter for all of us. Although my older brothers dropped out of school, they later married and moved. Two of them (Eugene and Gilbert) moved to Chicago to reside. The oldest one, Eugene, stayed in Chicago until his passing. Gilbert lived in Chicago for a number of years, then he relocated to Las Vegas, Nevada, where he still resides. My brother, George, the second oldest, remained in Arkansas until his demise. Carlton, my youngest brother, also moved to Chicago, after the military, married, and stayed in Chicago until his transition to eternity.

What I remember most about all of my brothers is how much we loved each other, our love for family and the Lord will always be one of my fondest memories. My brothers said my dad always told them. "Whatever you do, don't go too far, and don't stay too long." I was told that his advice was interpreted as: Do not go too far astray from the Lord, and do not stay away from Him too long. They are all forever in my heart...

John 16:22 - "And ye now therefore have sorrow: but I will see you again, and your heart shall rejoice, and your joy no man taketh from you" *(KJV)*.

Chapter 7

The Bridge

There was a lot of open space, dirt roads and land for miles and many, many bugs growing up in Arkansas. There were no interstate highways for a number of years, so prior to highways many of the roads ran through the small towns and counties that ran into the main traveling route 61. Route 61 runs North and South somewhat along the Mississippi River's path. In order to enter Tennessee, you must cross the bridge that goes over the Mississippi River. Now the Mississippi River, grand in size to anyone barely fifty pounds, and to a child - this river was massive! Just the same, the Memphis-Arkansas bridge allowed people to get across the states; and in a child's mind this bridge was just as rickety as the screen door that slammed shut from the kids running in and out of the house. To me, it seemed like we (my family and I) had to cross the river far too often for my liking.

Although Arkansas, specifically Chelford, was home to me I dreamed I would never have to cross the river or ever have to use the bridge to get to Memphis again. I wished I could snap my fingers and be wherever we needed to be; or that we just simply lived in Memphis to avoid the terrifying need to cross the bridge. Oftentimes, my siblings had to call me repeatedly to snap me out of my trances. An exceptional dreamer I was!

Obviously, one of my fears as a little girl dreamer was that I would have to dance a wicked dance with the Mississippi River and its guardian, the bridge. So, let us make the transition and start talking about me or how I came of this fear. It was at least once or twice on a monthly basis that we - my two younger siblings and one older brother - would accompany our dad, Bill, across the Mississippi River by way of the Memphis-Arkansas bridge into Tennessee to visit his brother and sister-in-law, our Uncle Gilbert and Aunt Hattie. The water in the river appeared to me, at that time, to be larger than the Pacific Ocean. Of course, I knew that rivers are smaller than oceans, but you could not have paid me any amount of money to believe that at this time of my tender youth and innocence to believe any body of water could be more intimidating or even larger than this river.

My dad would drive his old, brown two-door Chevrolet with us by his side to and from. I never wanted to sit in the front seat because I never wanted to see the river staring and laughing at me as I tried to dance calmly in my seat. My dance of pure sweat and shakes of nervousness were uncontrollable. I actually learned to pray during these road trips, while hiding on the floor of the car. "Please God don't let us fall into this river of water. I don't want to die on this raggedy bridge." Clearly each time we made it to Tennessee and back to Arkansas, I can only say it was by God's grace and mercy allowing us to cross that bridge so many times without any incidents or accidents.

Although I was fearful of the bridge and the water, I still loved visiting with my uncle and aunt. For a long time, I thought my uncle was a doctor because he had a small, black bag with medical supplies. Little did I know the bag held his medication for his diabetes. Something I know and understand now more with living. Makes me think of an expression my mother used to say: "You will understand, if God allows you to live long enough."

My aunt Hattie would always greet us with a big smile, lots of junk food and an enormous amount of love and warmth. She was easy to love, a high-spirited woman, round in size and skin buttery soft - perfectly suited for my uncle, in my opinion. At least I thought so. My uncle, he was a lot like my dad (his younger brother) – stern, hardworking, and always had a tight face as if he would never want to laugh. I learned later from one of my older siblings that my uncle and aunt had a son, Odie, who was killed on the railroad tracks in Tennessee along with his wife and child. I am not certain about the circumstances surrounding this incident of my cousins' death. I only heard it was a great tragedy during that time, so I started to pray for my aunt and uncle, and I prayed even harder when we crossed the Mississippi River. Although this was not the location of Odie and his family's death. I still made a comparison of my cousin's demise and what I would imagine their fear - to mine; and I was still afraid.

Subsequent to the death of my uncle, my aunt Hattie came to live with us. She was still feisty, although she walked with a cane. Her smile was infectious. In spite of our crowded conditions, I loved having my aunt Hattie with us. Since I was young, I was undaunted by the added responsibility for my parents. My aunt Hattie's feeble condition required much needed assistance. I did not consider the expense of food, clothing, sleeping arrangements (as I mentioned, with our current crowded conditions). During her stay, another challenge presented itself for my aunt Hattie. She started to become incontinent and the long walk to the outdoor restroom facility was simply too much to do, already on a cane. I remember one day getting off the school bus, and my aunt Hattie was struggling to make it to the restroom. I ran to assist her, but she did not make it. My dad (not taking the time to understand the aging process, or maybe upset by something else that happened in his day) was extremely upset with her. He reprimanded her saying, "Someone has to change you," and she started to cry. I, too, begin to sob uncontrollably. My tears were not for me, but for her helplessness as she got older. There's a saying that we are babies twice, and adults once - I now know the meaning. To have a chance to live a long life is a blessing, but it can also be hard on your loved ones to see as the elderly get older and slower. This episode was repeated many times in the future, and I believe the responsibility took a toll on my dad and my mom. I recall that my dad said Aunt Hattie had only one living relative, a brother, but she could not remember where he lived. My dad had to research the information she gave him to find her brother. Fortunately, my dad and one of my brothers were able to locate my aunt Hattie's brother, and she went to live with him. I cannot recall what happened to her after that.

Las Vegas - 2019

I had the opportunity to travel to Las Vegas to see my brother, Gilbert, and his daughter. I went along with my daughter, Yolanda and her son, Blake. We had a great time sightseeing so many wonders of the Las Vegas area. The flight was long; however, it gave me time to sleep and talk with my welcomed guest (my family). As soon as we arrived in Vegas, we could tell the temperature was drastically different than the Philadelphia weather. When we left it was 90 degrees and felt like 92. But, in Vegas, it was 110 degrees and just hot!

My brother lived right next to an elevated area of mountains that he used to walk through prior to getting older as we all seem to be doing. It's amazing how life slows you down, and we always seem to be in a rush to get older. Correction, we seem to want to rush to be an adult until being an adult gets real. We had an opportunity to ride around the area and see other family and friends that lived in Vegas; and I'm glad we did because as life should have it - I got a call some time later saying a family friend had the onset of early dementia.

As I said, we went sightseeing and just like when I was a child, I was a little intimidated seeing the massive size of the Hoover Dam as well as the Grand Canyon, yet this was different. I surmise my fear was not there now like it was as a child (crossing the bridge into Memphis) from first, my faith in the Lord and His protection over us and secondly because I was an adult, and much wiser. While at the Hoover Dam - it was amazing to see how there were two clocks that showed different times. One clock showed Pacific Standard time to represent the time on the Nevada side; and the other clock on the Arizona side displayed Mountain Standard time. Just the idea of time zones and seeing clocks to represent it side by side was mind blowing.

I was in complete awe of God's work and God's Work through people. Seeing the Bellagio fountain exhibit was great for me for the experience and just seeing how excited my grandson was! For anyone to have the ability to construct and engineer great works large and small must give God praise for that ability to think of it and see it through for others to enjoy. This was definitely beyond my imagination of how great it is to be able to see different parts of the world!

Chapter 8

The Well

My mother had two sisters and three brothers, but I only knew one brother. I remember her sisters - Viola and Larlene; and her brother - George. Her two brothers, Robert, and Emmanuel were deceased before I was born. I will always remember Mama's youngest sister Viola, of course whom I am named after. Aunt Viola was a tall, gorgeous (what people call) fair skinned woman that lived in Detroit, Michigan. She never had any biological children, but she did adopt a little girl. My mother's brother, George, lived in Osceola, Arkansas which was about 30 miles away from Joiner where we lived. Uncle George was the youngest in her family of brothers and sisters; and he had many children. I believe he had 18 children between his first and second wife. I was older than his second set of kids, so I wasn't as close to them growing up as the first set from his first wife.

My Aunt Larlene was my mother's oldest and closest sister. She also lived in Osceola, Arkansas and my mom visited her frequently. Of course, when my mom visited Aunt Larlene she took us (me, my two younger sisters, one older sister, and my youngest brother) with her for these visits. My brother, Gilbert, used to drive us to see Aunt Larlene because sadly, my mom never learned to drive. I guess she thought it was more important to raise her children and see to it that we were ok. My mom was selfless and looked out for everyone which explains why we went to help out.

Aunt Larlene had farm animals - pigs and a.horse. Whenever we visited, we found a way to agitate the horse. He would chase us because we saw fun in torturing him by throwing pebbles or sticks at him when we crossed into his fenced-in area. Whenever he saw us ('Lene (my sister), Carl, and me) nearing the fence he would charge full speed ahead and we took off running to safety to get to the other side of the fence.

We always got a kick out of being mischievous, really just having fun as kids do.

One day my mom and Aunt Larlene were milking the cows, and tending to the farm while my siblings and I decided to play around the well that was in my aunt's backyard. My brother wanted some water which made all of us want some. And for some reason, I thought it was a good idea to climb up on the well to fill the pail with water and try to pull it up for us to drink; but instead, I fell into the well. Just as I was plunging downward toward which I thought was my death, because I could not swim, I grabbed the rope that was used to lift and hold the pail when lowered in the well. To my advantage the pail was in the well, and I was tiny, so I was able to hold on to the rope while in the pail below.

My siblings yelled for help; I can still hear them saying "Viola is drowning in the well!" "Help, Jesus, Jesus, help! Viola fell in the water!" Of course, my aunt and my mother came running to rescue me from drowning. For me, I prayed, and I knew that God had plans for me, and he was my refuge. I was terrified the whole time counting the seconds which felt like minutes for my mom and aunt to pull me up.

Jeremiah 29:11 "For I know the thoughts that I think toward you, saith the LORD, thoughts of peace, and not of evil, to give you an expected end" (KJV).

Lord only knows how I didn't have a scratch on me once my mom and aunt pulled me out of the well. They thought for sure I was probably drowning because prior to getting to the well they thought the pail was resting on the well's hook where it normally is after each use. But God played a part and caused someone to keep the pail down this day. God knew my name!

Isaiah 43:1-2 "But now thus saith the LORD that created thee, O Jacob, and he that formed thee, O Israel, Fear not: for I have redeemed thee, I have called thee by thy name; thou art mine. 2 When thou passest through the waters, I will be with thee; and through the rivers, they shall not overflow thee: when thou walkest through the fire, thou shalt not be burned; neither shall the flame kindle upon thee" (KJV).

Tasha Cobbs Leonard and Featured artist Jimi Cravity sang it so beautifully a song entitled "You Know My Name."

As I reflect on this incident, I questioned why the Well was not covered, or enclosed within a gate to keep out underaged busy bodies (like me and my inquisitive siblings) as well as other unwelcome guests and creatures. The answers are– only God knows. He has a divine plan and purpose for all of our lives. He directs our paths, sets the course for our lives, and keeps us from drowning in the Wells we encounter daily. I urge you to think about a time when you felt you were in a Well of trouble, yet you can say as Timothy Wright "Trouble Don't Last Always."

Soon after this experience, my Aunt Larlene's son, Rufus, closed up the well area so that no one else would have a chance to climb on the well for water. I think we all praised God the whole way home for sparing my life. That experience caused Pain, but God had a Purpose to fulfill.

Chapter 9

Storm Shelter

I do have some fond memories of my childhood which I would not change for all the money in the world. The area where we lived in Arkansas was known for Tornadoes during certain times of the year. So, the fact that a storm had destroyed a house in the area where we used to live, my dad thought it was necessary to build a storm shelter for our new place of residence.

Just a quick sidebar before I give more details about this topic. I already shared that I walked slowly from my big shoes; but I also need to share that I ate slowly too. My siblings were always annoyed with me for eating slowly while reading a book or just daydreaming about something.

One evening, my dad received a message by radio and the meteorologist had forecasted a tornado warning in our area. We were having our supper when suddenly my dad said he saw evidence of the storm that was being discussed. There were (strong winds, heavy rain mixed with hail, thunder, and lightning. The tornado was heading towards us alright! We all had to go into the storm shelter immediately. The shelter was dark without electricity, but we had kerosene lamps which enabled us to see. We had to be very quiet when it was storming, and we were not allowed to do any activities either. My parents always said, "God is doing His work, and we should all be quiet." Since the storm came during dinner time and I had not finished my food - I decided to take my supper with me into the storm shelter, along with my milk which was my favorite drink. I remember sitting beside my oldest brother, with my plate on my lap, and slurping my milk so loud that it drew the attention of my siblings. Everyone started laughing at me and gave me the nickname of Bossie. Bossie was the name of the cow that came on tv for a milk commercial. So, because I drank so much milk and cows produce so much milk for people to drink, they thought the name suited me. It was really hilarious, and the name stayed with me for many years.

For the benefit of "city folk," anyone uncertain of what a storm shelter is - A storm shelter is an area of shelter (a hole) built underground for safety and its dimensions can vary. The storm shelter that my dad and brothers had for us was approximately 7'¾" inch wide and about 5 '1⁄2" long; I am guessing that it was 6 1/2 feet high and the steps were made of wood. The shelter's door consisted of tin and wood material to keep the rain from entering the inner safe space of the shelter. And the area inside the shelter had wood benches to sit on. My dad always kept a container with ice for food such as lunch meat and bread to make sandwiches, and there was also water. Since there was no electricity underground, we had kerosene lamps for lighting, and we kept blankets to cover ourselves.

While we sat through the storm, you could hear the rain pounding against the shelter door. The loud thunderous booms from the thunder and lightning were terrifying. In my mind, If I had to speculate, I would guess that the storm was a category 4. I know now and believe that "My soul has been anchored in the Lord." However, at that time, I felt like it may be the end of the world. I thought it could be another flood like in the Bible, and we would be under the ground for forty days without food or drink. I was young, so I never thought of how God had prepared His people for the flood. As I reflect back now, I know that God is so amazing! He always has a Purpose and a Divine plan when we had nothing, not a 'fore or afterthought on anything. But, Thank You Lord! I understand now that God can be trusted through the storms of life. I am confident that God's Word is an anchor that we can depend on.

An appropriate song that fits would be by Douglass Miller *"My Soul Has Been Anchored."*

Truly a testament for me and I am sure that many of the readers of this book can reflect on their own lives and have a testimony about God's Grace and Mercy. We received His favor! How many times He said, "Oh no, I already paid the price." Hallelujah! Somebody should say Amen!

I felt like God's work was truly scary and maybe we should be busying ourselves to possibly ease the fear of how loud he works. The booms and crashes actually sounded like God was bowling and getting many strikes! I then thought about the farm animals and the Bible. Should they have been in a storm shelter like in Noah's Ark? We were in the shelter, but where did the animals go? Were they going to be, okay? I bet they were scared and scrambling to avoid disaster as well.

After about forty-five long minutes, we all came out of the shelter to find destruction. The tornado did severe damage to our home. The front porch was ripped off (which was probably the boom we heard). There was wood and debris scattered around the yard, and the front window was shattered. There were small fragments of glass everywhere; and the screen door was swung open, but still intact.

After we gathered ourselves from surveying the damage, we started to clean up what we could. My dad and brothers did the heavy lifting, and the girls picked up the small pieces of trash to discard. I was saddened by all the damage and the fretful looks on my parents and older siblings' faces, however, I was also thankful. Thankfully, we were all safe. God was our refuge!

Chapter 10

Family And Friends

I have one friend that lived not too far from where my family and I lived in Chelford, Arkansas. We were the same age, and we also went to school together. There was so much she and I did together from being silly girls full of life to becoming saved girls still living life - at least trying to figure it out. As I think back over my life, I know I have done plenty of silly things and I am so grateful God has seen me through every childish thought and action. He kept me on my Journey through Pain for His Purpose.

I remember one time we (my friend and I) decided to go to the movies. And going to the movies during this timeframe meant segregated seating. Only whites were allowed to sit at the bottom of the theaters and blacks/coloreds had to sit above. The problem was we only had a little bit of money, and that little bit was not enough. We decided we would figure out how to get there and get in too. As we were walking down the road, we saw one of our neighbors and he asked us where we were off to. We fibbed and told him we were going to meet my daddy in town. He gave us a ride there and we thought he was going to just drop us off. But no. He was waiting for my dad to arrive, and we realized we had to tell the truth about where we were going. We also told him we did not have enough money to go to the movie either. Our neighbor was not happy with our decision once he learned our truth; however, he did give us the rest of the money and saw to it that we got back home safely as well. We were excited to know we had a ride back and enough money to get in, but just as he was getting ready to pull off he told us he was going to tell our parents that we lied and to make matters worse we did not have enough money to even go to see the movie - which meant we were going to try to sneak in.

We went into the movie theater and as we sat and watched I got too comfortable with us laughing at the movie and I took my shoes off. At some point I forgot my shoes were on the floor in front of me and when I went to stand, I accidentally knocked one of my shoes below in the white section of the theater. I was scared and just sat in disbelief not knowing what to do and reflecting on the consequences if I went to retrieve my shoe or if I got home without the pair. My friend and I saw our neighbor outside the theater, and he asked why I had only one shoe. Funny to me now, but not at the moment it transpired. Thankfully, my father was able to retrieve my shoe.

One night, I can recall that I went to visit one of my friends because her family had a color television. I can recall my mother explicitly telling me to be home before dark or sundown. She told me to be home because in rural areas, it was pitch black. There were no streetlights, houses were spread so far apart with dirt and/or rocky roads. The houses were what we called "a country mile" apart. Picture a dark deserted road, with no lights for a mile or almost a mile away. My parents had a flood light in the yard to mark our house and make it visible for people driving by or visiting. It was truly a significant difference between the city lifestyle with all streetlights and even the houses being close and some even rowhomes. This wasn't so in the country—not at that time at least. So, I stayed with my friend and her family until late and darkness seemed to creep in quickly with us watching tv. I realized time escaped and I had to go home in the dark.

I had to decide where to walk because on one side of the road there were cotton fields and on the other side of the road there were corn fields. The problem was after dark, more often than not, snakes would crawl across the fields and roads or just lie as predators in the field if anyone dared to walk through. So, I just walked in the street. After some time, I saw the headlights from a car approaching me and I was terrified since we (my friends and I) were told that someone had tried to kidnap a young girl from the road late one evening but was unsuccessful because of another road traveler. I was so afraid, from being told about the girl and not knowing if the story was real or not, that I ran into the cotton field where the cotton was high enough that I would not be visible to an oncoming traveler. God was my refuge, and I did not get bitten by a snake while in the field. I ran the rest of the way home, and my mother was waiting on the porch for me. She did not have a problem with me staying late ever again. I was a dreamer, but not irresponsible! I am confident that God knew my name even then according to His Word.

Psalm 139:9-11

"If I take the wings of the morning, and dwell in the uttermost parts of the sea: 10. Even there shall thy hand lead me, and thy right hand shall hold me. 11. If I say, 'Surly, the night shall cover me, and thy right hand shall hold me'" - (KJV).

Another experience I had a long time ago was when I was working at Yung's Chop Suey in Chicago, and when I got off work, I usually took a Jitney. A Jitney was a vehicle similar to today's Uber and Lyft. It was a mode of transportation less expensive than a taxi. However, on this particular day, unfortunately someone took my money that I put aside for my Jitney fare for me to get home after work. So, I dreaded the thought, but I was going to have to walk home. Thankfully, God worked it out. I am so grateful for my friend, Willie Lewis. Willie is a friend of mine from my childhood, that I grew up with in Arkansas. Like me, he came from a large family that was double the size of my family. There were 18 of them and he was number 14. I was number 7 of our 9. Similar to us and many families of the south - Willie and his siblings were born and raised in Arkansas; but they also migrated to various other states to include Illinois and Indiana. We had a lot in common and as life would have it, we parted ways and lost contact until the day at Yung's Chop Suey.

After so many years, Willie and I met again in Chicago, Illinois. (Remembering, God is Omnipresent, Omniscient and Omnipotent). He knew this situation would occur, so he prepared the way for me.

Psalms 23:5-6 "Thou preparest a table before me in the presence of mine enemies: thou anointest my head with oil; my cup runneth over. 6 Surely goodness and mercy shall follow me all the days of my life: and I will dwell in the house of the LORD forever" - *(KJV)*.

As I thought I would have to walk - Willie and his wife just so happened to come by the restaurant that night. It also so happens that his wife's aunt was married to the owner of the place where I worked. Willie and I always had a lot to talk about since we grew up together and lost contact over time. So, it was natural to always ask about each other's families. We knew the meaning of close-knit and extended family.

Eventually, Willie inquired about how I was going to get home, and I explained to him what I thought happened and that I did not have my money. I told him that I would have to walk from 75th and King Drive to 54th and Prairie Avenue. Immediately, he gave me money to take a Jitney for transportation home because they were heading in a different direction. I am thankful that Willie and his wife appeared when they did.

I have and had so many friends from my youth as well as my adulthood and all of them have made an impact in my life and some even in my family's lives. Unfortunately, I would rather not mention anyone else by name because as time should have it, I could not get their permission or their families' permission to mention them correctly and/or with full disclosure of some events. During the timeframe of writing these chapters I got really sick with renal failure taking over and it just made it more difficult to even attempt to mention everyone. Yet, I am grateful for the way God demonstrates His ability to take care of His own. He never, ever fails. God has shown Himself to be on time and mighty again when I was hospitalized in Indiana. And with this hospitalization, I was able to get Willie's permission to write about him and use his name.

Educational Opportunities

Dr. E. Beverly Young offered me my first higher education teaching experience. I was already teaching a Self Esteem, Problem Solving and Decision-Making course in the high school setting for the School of Social Work at Temple University. Dr. Young was a police officer for Temple University's Police Department. One semester she could not commit to teaching at the University of Saint Francis, so she referred me to the administration, suggesting I teach Crime and Society. The School of Social Work later asked me to teach a course called Institutional Racism; and I was also invited to be a guest lecturer at Wilmington, Delaware Urban Politics and Decision Making by Dr. Young (Bev). I have had an interesting Career in teaching higher education.

Wise Blessings

The Lord has put countless people in our lives as confidants, mentors, adopted moms and dads/pops, nanas, adopted sisters and brothers and we are so very grateful to each of you. Though many have transitioned on I have to mention someone who was so instrumental in assisting Elvis and I with our kids. Alice Woolard (affectionately known as Ms. Swoolabee/Ms. Woolabee to our family and kids) was our babysitter. She was truly a blessing in so many ways! Ms. Swoolabee was a reliable, dependable, faithful, God-fearing woman that embodied the true meaning of family friend, adopted mom/grandma, a babysitter, a Christian woman.

We were introduced to Alice Woolard by Elvis' brother, and his wife; and before long she was taking care of our children more so our youngest two, Yolanda and Addrena. Monday through Friday Ms. Swoolabee (that is what they called her) would walk the girls to and from elementary school, often having their friends tag along for the walk as well. My girls used to always ask, "Why does Ms. Swoolabee always wear long skirts and keep her head wrapped?," not realizing - that was a part of her religion as an Apostolic woman. To this day, I can recall so many times she would call the house to check in on us and leave the message saying her number was SA4-7098. Those were the days before 215 was necessary because we ran out of numbers; and SA stood for the numbers 72.

I can only shake my head to see how far we have come and how much times have changed. Ms. Swoolabee was old school! She grew vegetables in her backyard (greens, tomatoes, cucumbers, peppers, and onions) and would have the kids' snapping peas for dinner. She made hot water cornbread, chicken and dumplings, and apple dumplings like no other. We loved Ms. Swoolabee, and she adored us, the Malone family.

One day it seems Ms. Swoolabee (like many of us got older like the blink of an eye); and just like any day we called her to check in, but she did not answer all day and was not like her to do, so my daughter and I walked down the street to check on her. I'm thankful her daughter, Tina, entrusted us with a key. However, this evening we got to the house, and we just could not get in the house. It still pains me deeply because we could converse with her through the door, and we kept asking for her to open the door because our key would not work. I think it frustrated her more with us asking her to let us in and not realizing she had fallen and could not. I also do not know why we did not think to call an ambulance right then and have them try or kick the door in or something. But I guess it was not God's plan for us to get in because we would have never found out that Ms. Swoolabee was sick and had bedsores that were not healing. As a result, she was hospitalized and then went into a nursing home. I am thankful that God allowed her to see our daughter (one of her last two babies) graduate from college and walk in the nursing home with her cap and gown on. It was so exciting to see her face glow with joy as she called on the Lord and reached out for a hug, knowing she had a hand in this accomplishment - for it was not an easy feat for kids growing up in southwest Philly without getting in some sort of trouble. Alice Woolard was our blessing, our angel on earth that protected our children from hurt, harm, and danger; and I am saddened that she is gone, but according to:

2 Corinthians 5:8 "To be absent from the body is to be present with the Lord" (KJV).

Deacon Charlie James and his wife were dear friends to Elvis and me as well. We met them like we did many of our friends at Mt. Zion Baptist Church and our involvement in church activities. Deacon James was on the Board of Deacons with my husband, Elvis; and his wife was on the Deaconesses ministry with me. Mrs. James and I took turns hosting fellowship meetings for the deaconess members and we became better acquainted with one another allowing our friendship to grow; which allowed our husbands to socialize and fellowship more as well. Subsequent to Mrs. James' demise Deacon James relocated to Denmark, South Carolina his hometown. We (my family) continued to visit Deacon James at his South Carolina home. One time, I recall he took us to see a landmark Fort Sumter (which was only accessible by ferry), and we also went to see Hot Springs. Deacon James gave us a history lesson - telling stories of slave ports and he gave us a science lesson - showing us how to bait a hook and fish. Another time we visited John's Island, and the children were able to do more sightseeing and adventures. He was the great grandfather my children and grandchildren did not know. Deacon James drove to Florida to see and spend time with us and our grandchildren. We talked about countless bible stories and his love of the Lord. He and his wife were a praying couple.

As we visited Deacon James in South Carolina he introduced us to several of his family members over the years. We met his nieces and great nephews that did not live too far from him. They always greeted us and accepted us as extended family to Deacon James. There were many good times with the James family and for this I am grateful.

My Sisters and My Brothers

God has blessed me to have 4 brothers and 4 sisters - all whom I love dearly and appreciate even more for all they have done for me over the years. I miss my siblings that have transitioned to Glory, and I miss the ones that are still here now because of the traveling distance between us. However, this thanks is for you.

I thank you for innumerable times of joy and laughter; tough times; sadness, heartaches, and disappointments; family time, cookouts/reunions, sharing of secrets; encouraging words and not so encouraging words, but support none the less. I think often of my brothers and my sisters and how much I have learned growing and experiencing life with them close by and far away.

Eugene - my "Genio" - thank you for always being a big brother and giving more than you ever should have to. I remember you always giving somebody a nickname.

George - my playful, dancing, jokester - thank you for always looking out for us and being our protector. You were a hard worker and knew how to run heavy farm machinery. And man, could you dance!

Gilbert - my sweetie, thank you for always having a pleasant smile and welcoming spirit.

Emma - my oldest sister, thank you for being John's godmother and a great sister! You were the one who purchased my prom shoes and dress. Then later gave me a place to stay when I moved to Indiana. To this day, Emma even being in a nursing home in Florida continues to sing the Lord's praises and gives God the Glory for all things. Known to say in every situation "It is Well."

Carlton - my cool matchmaking brother, thank you for being the reason Elvis came to visit. I will remember you always wanting your head scratched.

Larlene- my songbird and prayer warrior, thank you for always keeping me on my toes. I remember us competing for who could pray the most; and we would up the number based on what the other one would say and go and pray.

Rosie - my sister of few words, thank you for always being kind, and soft spoken, a gentle spirit.

Henerietta - my baby sister, thank you for being one of my closest friends as we grow older and always giving me advice or suggestions, always showing patience and kindness.

I remember several family reunions and gatherings. The last reunion I can recall was in Jonesboro, Arkansas prior to the pandemic. My great niece did a great job spearheading this reunion and she did extensive research into the Jackson/Guy family history giving out trinkets and pictures of my mom and dad. I have a host of nieces and nephews that have done a great deal to show their Aunt Vye love and respect; valuing my opinion and insight on many topics and I love you all!

Proverbs 3:5-6 says, "Trust in the Lord with all thine heart, and lean not unto thine own understanding. In all thy ways acknowledge him, and he shall direct thy paths straight" (KJV).

I must admit this chapter on family and friends presents a conundrum for me. There are so many people, family, and friends that I would like to make mention of, pay tribute to give a shout out to, give kudos to, however, I may unintentionally neglect to mention one person or a few people that were kind and I do not want to do that. Still another reason I do not want to mention names is because so many of my friends have transitioned and I do not feel comfortable naming them. Therefore, I shall make limitations to writing the names of so many friends that have been there for me in so many ways. Just thinking about the list of states that I shared in my acknowledgement saying that I received some sort of communication, or gift from (many in less than a year). Imagine me not putting someone's name in this book to thank them for their kindness. I already explained/stated that I am not an ignorant!

What I do want to share is how grateful I am for the friends that came to visit with me, my husband, Elvis, and our family. There are so many of you that brought food to share, prayed with and for us, and offered plenty of support mentally. A thank you is just not enough. I cannot express the joy I feel for those friends that came to give us communion. If you are not familiar with the Baptist Church's hierarchy, a District Deacon is assigned to members of the church that live in a specified area. So, I am grateful to those Deacons that came to serve us, those that were within our district and those that were not in our District. Simply - their thoughtfulness will never go unnoticed.

I often think of the times that we have been invited out to breakfast, lunch, brunch, dinner, and supper with close friends. I would be remiss if I called the names of some and did not mention everyone. I am still in awe of the number of cards we have received over the past year. Most especially, there are ladies that frequently send beautiful cards with hopeful, inspiring, and encouraging messages. I do not want to embarrass you by mentioning your names; and I also know how modest you are; so, your cards to me and my family are appreciated, thank you. There are a number of ministers that I have a great deal of respect for; and they constantly display their love for people, friendship, integrity, and their love for God's Word. Some of them Pastor a church, and yet, because of their love for people and God, take the time to visit or call to pray and encourage others that may not be members of their church - to include me and Elvis and I am grateful. I wish I had your permission to write your names in this book. However, I am convinced that God looks at your heart and that your names are written in The Lamb's Book of Life.

When Life Gives Lemons

I was diagnosed with vitiligo in the summer of 1977. It started off as just a small light spot on my arm then it started to spread more and more. I got really depressed thinking I always had to cover my arms with long sleeves to protect my skin from the damaging sun. Often, I think I was covering up from my own discomfort from the condition or from people staring. I used to get so tired of people asking me if I was hot in the summer, but honestly having on sleeved shirts cooled my body from not having direct exposure to the sun. I can remember questioning God and even being somewhat angry about my skin getting worse over time and never getting better no matter how much I prayed. I was told by my family that God had chosen me as an example. My remarks were I don't want Him to select me for anything. Get somebody else to do His work. I eventually had to remember that some people are not granted or relieved of all things on this side and I am not ready for eternal life, so I won't complain.

Family Reunion Visit - September 2022

I guess this is the best time to discuss the awesomeness of God just recently! In September of 2022, I traveled to Illinois to meet with my family. The occasion was to celebrate my brother, Gilbert's birthday. He and his daughter were traveling from Las Vegas and Nevada to Illinois. Other members of the family would be traveling from other states and cities as well. So, the plan was for all of us to meet in Illinois. I arrived in Illinois at the Midway Airport on a beautiful day in September. My niece and her grandson picked me up from the airport and we had a wonderful time together. I was exhausted from the plane ride and a bit hungry. I expressed my hunger to my niece while she was cruising along a strip of fast-food places. There were so many choices, but I decided to get french fries to satisfy my appetite. Because I knew that my sister, Henrietta, would probably have food prepared and with her being an excellent cook - I looked forward to being a glutton. Father, forgive me. So, the fries had to do. My niece insisted on paying. After I gulped down the fries, I noticed my great, great nephew, my niece's grandson, awoke in the back seat. What a joy to see and hear him.

Finally, we arrived at Harry and Henrietta's home. Harry is my sister, Henrietta's husband. Once I arrived, what a reunion! We wept, we hugged, and we praised God for allowing us to come together one more time for something good. My great, great nephew was busy exploring my sister and brother-in-law's home because it is so lovely with much to take in. From the outside, their home appears to be a ranch, however it isn't. There are so many rooms and a basement that could be a two-bedroom apartment.

Harry is a genius who loves gadgets. I guess he is what's known as a techie. Everything in their home is modern and Harry assures that they stay up to date on all technical devices, and artificial intelligence. He amazes me. Harry and Henrietta allowed the baby to explore wherever he wanted to, and I followed, admiring all the decor and carefully thought-out interior designing of my sister. Harry and Retta make a great team. Henrietta has always had an eye for decorating and using space wisely. She has created an ambience of welcome, peace and comfort from the moment you pull into their circular driveway all the way to the outer portion of land they own. Retta even nurtures the wildlife (from a distance) that appear in the yard to get bread crumbs or other goods she leaves out. Often you see the birds, deer or even a small fox wandering around through her kitchen window that sits about the backyard's patio.

We (my great, great nephew, Retta, and I) walked all around the first level where the bedrooms are, the pool outside, the landscape in the front and the rear of the house looking at the beautiful flowers and plants. We walked through the Florida room, on the deck, the recreation room, the kitchen, the laundry area which led to the garage, and we backtracked back to the bathrooms. I was worn out and didn't have half the energy of this little guy. So, I went to get something to eat and sit with my family.

Surprisingly, my sister had not prepared food so we decided to order out for dinner and breakfast so we wouldn't miss any time with family cooking. The following morning, we had a hungry man's breakfast - bacon, sausage, pancakes, home-fries, grits, eggs, biscuits, toast, fruit, jelly, jam, cereal, juices, milk, coffee, and tea. All day we sat and talked and welcomed the company and family that came to visit us "out of towners."

Later that evening, we went out for dinner at a small family restaurant. I was on a vegan diet at that time because of my kidneys, so I had fried green tomatoes and fried okra with corn bread - a down home southern meal. My brother - Gilbert and his daughter arrived from Vegas soon after we finished dinner. We repeated the reunion sharing memories, life experiences and family updates. Just simply - Good times!

My brother, Gilbert, and I were spending the night at Harry and Retta's since they had the space, and we live so far apart we didn't want the night to end. My sister, Henrietta, and I stayed up to talk and reminisce about the past. We must have stayed up past midnight laughing, talking, and having fun remembering our deceased and living family and friends. I do not remember falling asleep at all with so much fun and laughter.

As God's will unfolded, I didn't wake up fully the next day. And just some humor all though a grave situation - Since I did not awaken the following day, I now know the importance of not going to bed angry. I cannot recall anything for the next 3 days and I did not eat for 3 days either. However, this is what I am told happened while God watched over me.

Thankfully, my sister and I fell asleep together. She, Henrietta, told me that she attempted to wake me in the morning, and she thought I was playing and pretending to be asleep. But after several calls and shakes, she realized I was totally unresponsive and not playing at all. She was, of course, very upset and called out to her husband, Harry, who called the rescue squad. I remained unresponsive even with medical assistance; however, my sister told me I moaned seemingly in pain when the medics touched my back and moved me. God was working His plan to have me in Illinois and not Philadelphia when this occurred. I was told I was taken to Franciscan Health Hospital's Emergency Department in Indiana, and the doctors immediately started working on removing toxins from my body due to kidney failure.

My family back home was awakened to a 7am eastern standard time call from their Aunt Retta. Drema (my oldest daughter) said she got the call from her Auntie a little after 7am and immediately knew something was wrong. She explained that she answered the phone and Henrietta said, "Hey Baby, It's Aunt Retta. Your mom is sick, and I can't wake her up." Drema told me that Retta said they called rescue and was waiting for them to get there; and that she would call her back when she knew more. Drema called her sisters and brother to let them know what was going on. Yolanda told me when Drema called her, she did not understand what Drema meant by saying "Mommy won't wake up" and during their call Retta called Drema back with updated information. Yolanda said shortly after Drema called everyone back with more details.

My children had to make a decision on saving my life with an emergency procedure and dialysis treatment. According to Henrietta, the doctors informed her that my kidneys had failed, and toxins were taking over my body and that my husband and children needed to grant permission for an access port to be placed in my neck in order for it to be done immediately. I only remember what I was told happened prior to when I awakened with a tube in my neck. Intentionally grateful because the Lord woke me up in time, and not in eternity.

The doctors, nurses, and the techs told me I repeatedly said, "Jesus, Jesus, Jesus." All I can say is I must have felt the Lord's presence if I kept making reference to Him. Similar to *the song "The Presence of the Lord is Here" by* Byron Cage. My children also told me I kept saying "Oh, Lord have mercy!" What I do remember is me inquiring why I have a tube in my neck and being told it was for dialysis treatment. I immediately said, "I do not want dialysis." I was told very pointedly that I had to have dialysis or die. Well, obviously, I chose to continue with dialysis. However, I want to be candid with my readers. I am not clear what God has planned for me and I am adjusting to dialysis as best as I can. While spending time in the hospital, I am so grateful for my family and friends praying, and laying hands on me, anointing me with oil, holding my hands and calling on the Lord to comfort me. My brother, Gilbert, my nieces and nephews, my sister and my friends were there in the hospital constantly praying and playing gospel music.

Matthew 18:19-20 "Again I say unto you, That if two of you shall agree on earth as touching anything that they shall ask, it shall be done for them of my Father which is in heaven. 20 For where two or three are gathered together in my name, there am I in the midst of them" - (KJV).

I thank God that my children decided that one of them should fly to Chicago because the doctors said the dialysis will clean out my blood and I should awake within 24 hours. They knew one of them needed to go and ascertain what was going on, be readily available to answer any health-related questions and make any calls on my behalf. It was really a touch and go situation and only God knew the outcome if their mother (me) was in fact going to be okay. My children decided that my sister, Henrietta, needed assistance because she already had so much on her with her own family's needs. Some may know, my middle daughter, Yolanda, was the representative to fly to Chicago to help with me and I am told she landed, and I woke up almost at the same time. My niece called her (Yolanda) as she was walking to the departure area of the airport to let her know where she was parked and that I was coming around to be responsive. Yolanda told me my niece brought her straight to the hospital. My other children, John, Drema and Addrena had their roles to play, especially assisting with their father, Elvis who is disabled from a stroke, and maladies from the military. My other children were getting all of my medications and doctors' names and contacts in order, if and when they should be needed. They also told me they decided not to tell Elvis what was going on so as not to worry him before they could truly explain what was going on with me.

Still not feeling my best as I started to come around and it was just 24 hours after the emergency dialysis, I remember thinking that I was either dead or dreaming when Yolanda walked into my hospital room. Yolanda told me she asked if I knew who she was and I responded yes, but at the time she said I didn't call her name and was in and out of sleep. That night I was told I feared going to sleep because of the night before and all that happened, so my daughter stayed past visiting hours to comfort me and ease my fears. She told me that she kept reading the bible verses from the handkerchief that she had laid over my chest and she played gospel music too. Yolanda reminded me that I repeated "I shall not die, but live."

Psalm 118:17-18 "I shall not die, but live. And declare the works of the LORD. 18 The LORD hath chastened me sore: But he hath not given me over unto death" (KJV).

The next day my daughter came into my hospital room to visit, and she said she asked me again if I knew who she was - and she told me on day 3, I called her name and said, "Yes, you are my daughter, Yolanda." Yolanda also told me there was a tv mounted on the wall across from my bed that flashed a symbol of Jesus hanging on the cross and it also flashed a live video feed of the hospital sanctuary that had a cross and an altar. She told me that I would not let anyone stand in front of the tv because I would say they were blocking Jesus. I was told I kept saying "God is here, and I can see his face on the tv." Some of the nurses disregarded what I was saying, but Yolanda reminded me if God can talk to Moses through a bush why can't he talk to you through the tv.

Exodus 3: 2-5 "And the angel of the LORD appeared unto him in a flame of fire out of the midst of a bush: and he looked, and behold, the bush burned with fire, and the bush was not consumed. 3 And Moses said, I will now turn aside, and see this great sight, why the bush is not burnt. 4 And when the LORD saw that he turned aside to see, God called unto him out of the midst of the bush, and said, Moses, Moses. And he said, "Here am I" - (KJV).

I stayed in the hospital for several days and was dismissed with a walker and having dialysis 3 times a week. I was not strong enough to fly back to Philadelphia, so my daughter and I stayed at my sister's and Harry's for the rest of the month of September. I remember being fearful of going to sleep when it was time to go to bed, probably because this was my first night back at my family's house since I was hospitalized. I did not want to sleep alone, so Yolanda slept with me every night although I'm sure she did not want to. But she never voiced it, nor did she complain. One night, Yolanda went into the basement, and it worried me so much that I called her after about 20 minutes to tell her to come upstairs. Again, I guess because I was in the basement with Retta when I did not wake up and the thought of my child (although an adult) being in the basement by herself frightened me. I know how fearful I was going back to my sister's house, and I can only imagine and talk to my loved ones about how they felt. My family in Philadelphia having me being so far from home and having my kidneys fail; or my sister's view of waking up next to me and not being able to awake me or get a conscious response. No words can express my gratitude to all of them for everything they did but thank you!

To this day, I am still undergoing dialysis or renal therapy as I like to call it and having to endure surgery after surgery because of different roadblocks with having dialysis. Initially, the whole process was taking a toll on me mentally and emotionally. I guess just the whole ordeal; and not getting things such as healing on my time - has been a lot. When I started going to renal therapy, I could not understand why the facility was not set-up for patients to have a sense of privacy, a standard assigned seat and room or at least a partition to section people off. I also felt there should be an assigned nurse, tech, and daily renal doctors just for the what ifs. I sometimes still want to have an assigned seat, but I am better adjusted to having different techs as well as nurses. Admittingly, it works in my favor to have them switch up because it allows me to establish a rapport with them; and truthfully, I now even have favorites. "Don't judge a book" is so true, because the people at my facility are all different and care for me differently, as well. Some are attentive and caring, and others let's just say - hopefully, God will soften their hearts to love or even want to do what they do (their job) when caring for others.

Either way, I am maintaining it is all in God's time on all things! By staying true to His word while praising the most high for all the ways he has been my rock, my refuge, and my God with unchanging hands. Still on my Journey through Pain for God's Purpose.

Isaiah 41:10 "Fear thou not; for I am with thee: be not dismayed; for I am thy God: I will strengthen thee; yea, I will help thee; yea, I will uphold thee with the right hand of my righteousness" - (KJV)

I cannot end this without talking about my husband, Elvis and our four children, John, Drema, Yolanda and Addrena. Although they have their own children and other responsibilities, they have been exceptionally supportive of me and their father, Elvis. So, I think this is a perfect juncture for me to talk about them.

My Husband - Elvis

I met Elvis when I was 12 years old and starting high school. I was well developed physically, at that age, and academically prepared, but not sophisticated enough for high school. Elvis and I became good friends over time, and our upbringing was very similar. We could not date because of my age. However, he started coming to see my brother, Carlton. That was his excuse to see me. How clever! That was my Elvis, always clever! This plan continued until I was 14 years old. We would do homework together and meet every day in school. When I was 15, Elvis took me to our Junior Prom and the following year we went to our Senior Prom together, too. We shortly after graduated from high school. I was only 16 years old when I graduated. Our paths separated briefly because Elvis left for Indiana to prepare for medical school, and I left for Missouri to live with my dad's sister. I wanted to attend nursing school, at least at the time. I did not stay there long because I realized that I was not cut out for a healthcare career. I thought if he is going to be a doctor, then I should be a nurse. So, not so! I did not like needles, and I fainted when I saw blood! So, I moved to Indiana with my oldest sister, Emma, her husband and two children at that time. I was back and forth between my sister Emma's, my brother Gilbert's, and my brother Carlton's in Chicago. I am indebted to them as I was able to graduate from Cortez Peters Business School in Chicago. Elvis could not afford medical school, due to the economy. So, he enlisted in the United States Air Force. He did several tours before he came back to the states to Omaha, Nebraska. I was still in Indiana when Elvis proposed to me, and I accepted his proposal. We married in Omaha, Nebraska. Elvis was always an arduous worker. While in the military, he also worked another job and I worked for Omaha, Nebraska Airport. After a short time, we moved to Fairbanks, Alaska. We lived there for a few years and our oldest daughter, Drema, was born there. One of Elvis' co-workers had two boys and said if she ever had a daughter, she would name her "Drema." Needless to say, she never had a girl and she asked if we would name our daughter "Drema." We already had our son, John (he was born in Chicago), and we were not sure if our child I was carrying was a girl or a boy; but we agreed to the request.

We had many jobs while in Alaska. As mentioned, Elvis worked a second job while serving his military duty in Alaska; and I worked for the Alaska Water Laboratory. We lived in an apartment waiting for base housing. Once we moved into base housing, I started working at the Fairbanks Hospital. It took time and we had to adjust to the climate and time difference - 6 months of daylight and 6 months of darkness. It was a different kind of darkness and daylight. We had to adjust to the freezing temperatures and heavy snowfalls as well. Elvis purchased an Escomo Parka for me to wear in the cold. (All the friends/associates we acquired while in Alaska were Caucasian with the exception of one couple). This was the norm at both our places of employment. Elvis belonged to a Citizens Band (CB) Club. We, all the wives, had CB's to keep in touch with our husbands due to the inclement weather. This gadget was similar to a walkie talkie. It was very useful. At this particular time of course, there were no cell phones. Thank God for technology! Even after we left Alaska, (Elvis' final tour in the military) we remained in contact with two of the couples. One couple transferred to New Jersey, and the other couple transferred to Texas. We communicated with the couple in Texas through telephone and via mail; and the couple from New Jersey, we actually visited frequently.

Elvis had a job offer when we moved to Philadelphia from Alaska. His brother Bobby and his family were already living in Philadelphia when we arrived. Johnny, Elvis's youngest brother was also already living in Philadelphia. We lived with Bobby, his first wife and two children for 4 months until we found the home where we still reside. That has been over 50 years ago and we have had some challenges, to say the least, but we are grateful for perseverance.

Prior to Elvis having a stroke he participated in many events with our children and their children. Taking much pride in being a grandfather, going on school trips and always on a council for parents on how to improve the schools the children attended. He was supportive of me working during the day at Temple University while working on my PHD; and he worked nights and sometimes days too. Elvis was also a member of the board for Mercy Douglass Human Services for many years; and he was very instrumental in the neighborhood doing community events and providing political awareness to adults and children.

Our Children:

We are blessed with 4 children that have contributed to our family in their own ways and we are thankful. All of them have their own children and have their own stories to tell. But I will say each of them have their own personality and spunk only sharing a common love of the Lord and love of family. They are all very close even being spread out in ages.

John

John, our only son and the oldest of our four children, has been instrumental in helping out daily with me and Elvis in spite of being in and out of the hospital with medical challenges. He was diagnosed with sickle cell disease when he was an infant; and yet his illness did not inhibit him from participating in extracurricular activities while growing up. John attended Temple University - lived on campus and had many experiences while in school. He left Philadelphia with his uncle to visit family in Illinois, and later he enrolled in Defy University. When John returned home to Philadelphia, he gained employment at Independent Blue Cross and remained there for approximately 19 years until he came out on disability. He started helping with family responsibilities over 17 years ago when Elvis became disabled. Recently, he has been assisting with Elvis and taking me to dialysis (renal therapy). John has managed to take full responsibility for his older children even with his own health condition. He has also been very helpful with taking us out to dinner or shopping just to have a change of scenery from time to time.

Drema

Drema, our oldest daughter, began working at Mercy Douglass Human Services when she was 17 years old as a physical therapy aide and worked as she completed her bachelor's degree from Temple University Fox School of Business. She started nursing school, but discontinued when Elvis became disabled. Drema later enrolled at St. Joseph's University and completed her Master's Degree in Health Care Administration. She assisted with the care of Elvis, and when I had renal failure, she started taking me to dialysis. Drema has always been a reserved individual that accepts responsibility without complaining. Drema has her health challenges but manages to help others. She assumed the management of Elvis and my invoices while working a full-time job, raising her daughter, who is now enrolled in Holy Family University for her Bachelor of Science in Nursing - BSN. Drema still checks on the family. She is employed at Mercy Douglass Human Services Affiliate as the Property Manager Supervisor. Drema has always been one to make sure we are comfortable and taking the right doses of medication. She continues to be a point person talking to the doctors and/or nurses to make sure we are on track.

Yolanda

Yolanda, our middle daughter, completed her bachelor's degree from Temple University College of Arts in Psychology. After completion of college, she started working in the mental health field as a Therapeutic

Staff Support worker for Children's Outreach under the Resources for Human Development. Noticed for her positive interactions and care for students, the school's vice principal encouraged her to go back to school for her masters under the Balanced Literacy Intern program with the Philadelphia School District. She later enrolled at St. Joseph University and received her Masters Degree in Elementary Education. Yolanda has been teaching school for over 22 years and she just recently passed her PreK-12 Special Education Praxis for certification. Yolanda had a serious health challenge in 2018; but that is her story which I will not share in this book. Yolanda loves to cook and is very good at making healthy, exotic dishes, trying exciting new recipes, and caring for her two sons. Yolanda has been helpful in caring for me and Elvis–cooking, shopping, taking me to dialysis, and spending the night to help with chores.

Addrena

Addrena, our youngest, completed her bachelor's degree from Temple University's Fox School of Business. She was also employed at Mercy Douglass Human Services in the medical records department. A family friend and co-worker guided and mentored Addrena into property management. This gave Addrena 23 years of property management experience leading to her receiving several Housing Designations. She also has a Real Estate Salesperson License in Pennsylvania and New Jersey. Addrena has one daughter that she adores, and they both come over frequently to assist with caring for me and Elvis. She ensures that I have a ride to and from dialysis on days her siblings cannot all the while working from home and caring for her daughter. She always brings household items and food to the house, buying double what she gets to make sure we are fully stocked with toiletries, juice, and water.

I am thankful for my family and my immediate family. God knows exactly what we need when we need it. My children told me they felt I should not have gone to Illinois and that I pushed myself to go. But they soon realized that God needed me to be in Illinois in order to save my life. If it were not for me and my sister sleeping in the same bed that evening, who knows if I could have finished this portion of the book.

Only God knows! Therefore, I will not question and only stay dutifully in prayer and grateful for all blessings. Truly knowing the song by "He Keeps on Blessing Me."

Church Affiliation

Elvis and I are members of The Mount Zion Baptist Church located at 1415 S. 50th St., in southwest Philadelphia. We have been members of Mt. Zion since moving to Philadelphia and we served as Deacon and Deaconess throughout the years. Much like our parents we have guided our children and without fail showed them faithfulness in serving God. Our children have participated in many events at the church such as Vacation Bible School, Speaker's Contest, Poster Contest, Ushering Ministry, the Gospel heirs singing group, Carnation Choir, Sunday School, and countless banquets.

I have thoroughly enjoyed participating in all the church activities– some of them with my children and others with my husband. I felt a great deal of satisfaction having been instrumental in assisting with the Library and instituting literacy classes for persons wanting to finish high school, or complete a GED, or simply wanting to improve their language skills.

I sorely miss the Business and Professional Women's Christmas socials. We had so much fun with our chairperson playing Santa Claus. She was delightful. It will never be forgotten how the Deaconess' visited with our husbands to commune the sick and shut-in. There is a lady in my church that reminds me of the President of the United States' first lady. She does not think so, but her manners are much like the former first lady. I can never forget the Boy Scouts and the Girl Scouts. Wow! Sunday School, what a joy, teaching, learning, and watching the children learn and grow.

There are so many other lasting memories. I remember all of the pastors of Mt. Zion Baptist Church, with the exception of the founding pastor. I am grateful to have known each preacher/pastor.

Reverend Dr. Willie E. Robinson was our previous pastor at Mt Zion to whom I am grateful for because he was an unwavering shepherd during my children's time of need (especially my girls), when my husband had a stroke. He prayed with them exhibiting faith and strength and he encouraged them to keep the faith that their father was going to live and not die. I felt stronger after his prayer of encouragement in the hospital with us. I shall never forget his congregation song, I Love You Lord."

To his wife, Mrs. Robinson, I am grateful for her unselfishness. She has always been dear to me and my family and to the church, always giving her time, faith and exhibiting leadership within the Women's Fellowship. I will always value her friendship and guidance.

Our current pastor, Rev. Cedric H. Jones, Jr. has a unique personality and style of preaching. He is intelligent, a teacher, preacher, articulate and filled with the love of God for his congregation. I remember Pastor Jones transitioning into the Mt. Zion family and he made his first efforts to visit with the seasoned deacons of the church to include Elvis. I am grateful for his prayers and concern for me and my family during my time of illness.

Self Care

I have written so much about my friends and family that I feel like I need to speak a little about my own likes even as an adult, a wife and mother. All of my experiences have created an opportunity for me to be more and more appreciative of life and living. There are so many things I had a chance to do as an adult and I realize that I like to ski, roller skate, bowl and play family games. A good movie at the theater or home is always a great way to pass time with family or alone in the comfort of my home. A musical or play is always nice to go see as well. I wanted to learn how to play the piano, so I made sure my children were exposed to music. I have learned that I like different genres of music, and I used to dance, and I still like to go to the center to line dance from time to time. Education has always been dear to me, so whenever I was asked to teach I would. I also joined an educational sorority and completed community work with them. My family is important to me and has had an impact on me and my views of life; but most importantly I have learned I have to live for me and enjoy the blessings God has bestowed upon me.

Acknowledgments

I am grateful to God, my family and friends from so many states (Illinois, Indiana, California, Nevada, Wisconsin, Minnesota, Tennessee, Texas, Florida, Alabama, Georgia, Arkansas, Pennsylvania, Ohio, Delaware, Virginia (I was unable to get permission from my friend from Virginia to mention her name), New Jersey, and Connecticut), for the care and support I received and continue to receive throughout my life and especially over the last few years. I cannot express the joy, and hope I felt from all of your prayers, visits, flowers, cards, food, monetary and other means of support to me and my family. I am humbled to say the least. I am afraid to write any names of all the countless people that I would like to call. First, it would consume too many pages and secondly, I may unintentionally, leave someone off that did an act of kindness and/or that gave me hope.

Thank you to my family and friends in Illinois and surrounding areas that came to visit me during my hospital stay. Thank you for praying over and for me. Again, I thank my sister, Henrietta, and her family for opening their home to me and my daughter, Yolanda for 2 weeks as I recuperated after being discharged from the hospital. No words can express my gratitude - from calling the ambulance to save my life, allowing Yolanda to use your car to go back and forth to the hospital and/or transporting me to dialysis treatment; and to do so many other countless things. Retta, I cannot imagine the scare that I had given you, but it was God's plan, and I thank you - my sister, my friend. Thank you for having your church family and pastor pray for me and pray for us all! I would like to acknowledge and thank my daughter, Yolanda, for coming to Illinois and staying with me. Just you leaving your family and taking the time off of work speaks volumes and I appreciate you. There was nothing easy about getting up to take me to early morning dialysis appointments, cooking for me, and completing your homework for your certification classes. I am also appreciative of you taking so much time to discuss, edit and read countless times over my work.

I would like to thank Pastor Cedric H. Jones, Jr. for the prayers and support offered to my family during my hospitalization.

Thank you to Rev. Gail Johnson for penning the Forward for this book.

There is so much more to share, however, the publisher has been waiting for more than 4 years for this section of this book and I do not want to delay the process any longer. It has been delayed enough with the ongoing pandemic and other atrocities. Given that, I think I will bring closure to this book. Perhaps there will be another narrative in the future. It is time for a new narrative on many subjects.

Again, I cannot give enough accolades to my family, extended family, church family and friends. Thank you, Reverend Yolanda Johnson, for giving me the opportunity to pen this script with you. Forever so grateful - Dr. Viola J. Malone!

DISCLAIMER

Some of the readers were probably afraid to indulge in this reading because of my academic credentials, having a PHD and possibly expecting a dissertation and defense. Perhaps by now you know this is not about academia and I have and had a life prior to a PHD. In fact, this narrative is a composition of some events and information about my life - long before any academic achievements. It is about my journey of struggles and challenges while growing up in a rural area in the deep South all the while knowing to look to and for God for help in all things. I tried to write so that any reader can understand, process, and have a dialogue with others. And for anyone interested in my academic career and that part of my life feel free to reach out. Let's have a conversation at a mutually agreed time in the future. Maybe I'll bring some milk - a little more humor. But with all hearts and minds being clear - In Jesus Holy Name - Amen!

References

The Bible. The Open Bible King James Version (KJV) Published by Thomas Nelson as part of HarperCollins Christian Publishing, Inc. Thomas Nelson is headquartered in Nashville, TN.

2 Corinthians 5:8
Exodus 3:2-5
Isaiah 41:10
Isaiah 43:1-2
James 5:16 - KJV
Jeremiah 29:11
John 16:22
Matthew 18:19-20
Proverbs 3:5-6
Proverbs 12:11
Psalms 23:5-6
Psalms 46:1
Psalm 91
Psalms 113:3
Psalm 118:17-18
Psalms 139:9-11

Barnes, L. (2007). You Keep on Blessing Me. [Luther Barnes]. You Keep on Blessing Me.

Brown, B and Cobbs-Leonard, T. (2017). You Know My Name [T. Cobbs-Leonard and J. Cravity]. Heart. Passion. Pursuit.

Brown, S. (2005). Grateful [H. Walker]. The Essential Hezekiah Walker.

Caesar, S and Mathis, M. (1989). I Remember Mama [S. Caesar]. I Remember Mama.

Carr, K. (2006). The Presence of the Lord is Here. [B. Cage]. Live at New Birth Cathedral.

Gaither. B. (1963). He Touched Me. [Bill Gaither Trio]. He Touched Me.

Miller, D. (2003). My Soul has been anchored in the Lord. - [Douglass Miller]. Unspeakable Joy.

Sapp, M. (2007). Never Would Have Made It. [M. Sapp]. Thirsty.

Williams, F. (1993). Your Grace and Mercy. [The Mississippi Mass Choir, Featuring F. Williams]. It Remains to be Seen.

Wright, T. (2009). Trouble Don't Last Always [T. Wright and The Chicago Interdenominational Mass Choir]. I'm Glad About It.

This poem was submitted by one of our beloved friends who loves Seniors. It reflects the love that we have for our families, friends, and loved ones, we hope you are encouraged by the reflections and journey in life enveloped with pain that led to our purpose.

Thank you, Reverend Sanders, for the two poems submitted with love.

Light and love by remember DonovIn. Reverend Jerry Sanders author

Light and love are complementary.
A harmony unmatched by a masterpiece symphony
Love is the fountain from which light springs.
The light of love shines the way to good things.
Love and light are aspects of each other.
Light is produced when we love one another.
Love and light are wholesome and refreshing.
God's light and God's love are the ultimate blessing.

Printed in the United States
by Baker & Taylor Publisher Services